THE WEALTH MASTERY PLAYBOOK

THE REIN PRESS

The REIN Press publishes informative and thought-provoking content on real estate investing, finance and personal finance. The authors are leading educators and practitioners in their respective fields.

With the advent of powerful search engines, the consumer has a bewildering amount of information to review in order to come to an informed decision. The publications of the REIN Press are designed with the consumer in mind: to offer clear, accessible content that has been tried and tested, thereby saving the consumer time and effort in the pursuit of knowledge and understanding — and ideas that work.

The
WEALTH
MASTERY
Playbook

The Six Essential Shifts
to a New Financial Destiny

RICHARD DOLAN

REIN Press
TORONTO • VANCOUVER

Books may be ordered in bulk quantities by contacting the publisher at 905.856.9243.

Library and Archives Canada Cataloguing in Publication

Dolan, Richard, 1974–
[Make your move]
      The wealth mastery playbook : the six essential shifts to a new financial destiny / Richard Dolan.

Previously published under the title Make your move.
ISBN 978-1-927432-10-5 (paperback)
ISBN 978-1-927432-11-2 (ebook)

      1. Finance, Personal. I. Title. II. Title: Make your move.

HG179.D64 2015   332.024   C2015-905277-7

Editorial Management: Loney Publishing Group Ltd., Toronto
Editors: Nicole Langlois and Lindsay Humphreys
Author photo: Stacey Barry/Azureblue
Cover image: iStock
Design & production: Counterpunch Inc/Peter Ross

The REIN Group of Companies
34B-8611 Weston Road, Vaughan, ON L4L 9P1
27520 58 Crescent, Unit 6, Langley, BC V4W 3W7
www.reincanada.com

First printing
Printed in Canada by Marquis on FSC® certified paper

CONTENTS

SHIFT 6

Design Your Greater Purpose   171

AFTERWORD

Be Resolute   187

APPENDIX

Quick Reference of Key Takeaways   189

ABOUT THE AUTHOR

Richard Dolan Entrepreneur, Author & Performance Strategist   192

FOREWORD

I was honored when my good friend and business partner Richard Dolan asked that I write the foreword for this, his latest book.

As a serial entrepreneur for over thirty years, a real estate investor, a business partner and more, I have learned valuable lessons (some the hard way) for creating and growing wealth. Now, having lived beyond the half-century point of my life's journey, I have found that the most important financial lessons I've learned were gained while attending the University of Life.

I have learned, for example, that building wealth and having the financial certainty and sense of security we all seek at some level is not really as complicated as most of us tend to believe.

Firstly, and at the risk of stating the obvious, building your financial foundation requires that you generate more income than what you spend. So whether you earn money in the public or private sector or are an entrepreneur with a small business, wealth is gained by generating revenue, spending less than you earn and investing wisely.

Seems simple enough — but as the saying goes, creating wealth IS simple; it's just not easy.

And that saying may in fact be your best reason for reading this book. Because secondly, what I have learned is that in order to create wealth and the life of your dreams you must understand your relationship with money and have a mindset consistent with building wealth.

As I studied the chapters of this playbook, I was inspired by the mastery with which Richard asks the right questions to help define the path to setting and meeting your financial goals. With clear language and inspiring examples and stories, Richard takes you on a process of self-discovery that will reveal who you are in terms of your relationship with money and wealth.

In order to achieve your financial goals, you must recognize the real value inherent in three things: your time, your energy and your knowledge. You must also recognize the things that are derailing you or will at some point stop you on your path: the decisions you make; the distractions you allow to happen; and your reactions to life events and, most importantly, what drives them.

These are the key considerations with respect to your relationship with money. They make the critical difference between the wealth you hope to accumulate and what you will accumulate.

To reach the milestones along the path of fulfilling your dreams and the dreams of others, wealth is the fuel but, as Richard says, the engine is your mind. He uses that metaphor to illustrate critical mindset shifts you must make to rid yourself of old belief systems, unprofitable habits and learned behaviors. Each shift is a call to action to prepare you for your new relationship with money, one that includes having clarity of intention and an unwavering commitment to achieving the result and the outcomes you want.

We are defined by adversity and challenge; as Henry Ford famously said, "Whether you think you can or think you can't — you're right." If you see challenges as things that are holding you back, they will hold you back. But if you shift your mindset — in other words, see challenges as a way to stretch into possibilities — then nothing can stop you. Success stories are born as a result of individuals reaching beyond the limitations of what they thought was possible to achieve what actually became possible.

Keep your playbook close at hand, as it will serve as both your personal guide and North Star to help you navigate through life's uncertainties to a financial future free of compromise and uncertainty.

Patrick Francey
CEO, REIN

CREATE A WEALTH MASTERY MINDSET

There is a door behind which lies a vast treasure. This door cannot be breached by physical force; no explosive can mar its immaculate face, and no form of thievery will force the lock. Only possessing knowledge of the code will unlock the door and reveal the treasure within.

There is no computer that can decipher the code, and no army that can force the door from its hinges. Without the code, the door remains firmly locked to all. And to the great masses of people, the treasure may seem to remain a fantasy, forever out of reach and never to be exposed. But with a benevolent and charitable spirit, the giants of history have seen fit to pass the code down through time so that it is within the grasp of all.

Where is this impassable door, you ask? And where can the code be found? The door through which you must pass to all the wealth you could ever desire, all the riches you could even imagine — is your *mind*.

Shift Your Mindset

If you knew you could not fail, what would you attempt? Answering this question requires much courage because it means facing your fears and admitting what is deep in your heart, what you truly desire. This true desire is accompanied by fear — a fear of failure. There are things you dream of around which fear has erected a barrier. You know that you are fearful and that fear has stopped you. You should feel proud to admit that there are things you desire that you have not yet attained, that still linger unfulfilled in your imagination. Don't brush these thoughts aside! They are fertile seeds of possibility that need only the nurturing waters of belief to bring them to life.

In 1975, a 29-year-old struggling actor from New York realized that he needed to create a role for himself. He needed to promote himself to the world, and so he resolved to write, direct and star in his own movie. This would be no easy feat, considering how emotionally debilitating his financial situation was. He lived in a run-down apartment beside the subway, barely had money for food and was struggling to make rent. He was up one night watching a boxing match on television when inspiration hit. He wrote day and night for the next three days to create a script, and then he began shopping it around to movie studios.

To his great delight, studios loved it! But they didn't want him to be the lead actor. They wanted to cast someone with star power, a proven draw at the box office. And so this struggling actor was offered $350,000 for the rights to the script. He was desperate for money to make rent, and that amount was a small fortune to him. But this young actor and writer was possessed with no ordinary dream. He was consumed with a burning desire to become a major Hollywood star, and he knew he had to be the lead. And so Sylvester Stallone turned down the money and held his ground. He eventually got his wish. *Rocky* came out in 1976 with Stallone in the starring role, and the rest is history.

Be Committed to Personal Growth

If you aren't sure whether you could cross the finish line to achieving wealth, ask yourself if you are the type of person who is at least able and willing to run. Ask yourself what you would be willing to do if attaining your goal were possible. Would you be willing to work hard? Would you be willing to invest time in your business? Would you be willing to be subject to rejection and ridicule? Would you be willing to learn and change and become the very best person you can possibly be? What are some of the things about yourself, your character and your conduct that you know can be improved? If you are committed to hard work and self-improvement, what goal couldn't you eventually attain? If you were totally committed to becoming the best person you can be, mastering the skills required and putting in the hours, what goal on earth would be beyond the reach of a person as powerful as you?

One man who was committed to personal growth was Sir Edmund Hillary, the first person to climb Mount Everest. He completed his goal on May 29, 1953. However, his successful summit was not his first attempt, for he had tried and failed in 1951. Nonetheless, the British Parliament decided that some sort of award should be presented for his near-completed attempt. At the ceremony honoring him, a picture of Mount Everest was projected on the wall. When the award was presented, the crowd rose for a standing ovation. Hillary walked over to the picture looming above him. Turning to face the picture and shaking his fist at it, he shouted, "Everest, you defeated me! But you won't defeat me again! Because you have grown all you can grow ... but I am still growing!"

As long as you are committed to working hard and continuously improving, you too can become the type of person who accomplishes the goals you desire.

Believe that It's Humanly Possible

You may doubt your own abilities, but can you conceive that the goal you have for yourself is possible within the realm of human achievement? One of the surest ways of building belief is to recognize the multitude of successful examples that surround you. If you have the desire to earn $1 million a year, ask yourself: Does anyone make a million dollars a year?

The answer, as you know, is *yes*. How many people do this? Millions of people in North America alone. Are they necessarily smarter than you? Maybe not. I remember hearing in high school that the "A" students become professors to teach the "B" students to become employees who work for "C" students that own businesses. The message here is that receiving good grades in school is no predictor that you will be a millionaire.

What about hard work? Sure, you're going to work hard. I remember a guy once saying to me, "I'm self-employed and only work half days — but I get to choose which twelve hours I work!" If you want to become wealthy, you can count on working at a higher operational tempo than an employee who checks out emotionally at 8 a.m., checks out mentally at 2 p.m. and checks out physically at 5 p.m. People who become wealthy aren't chasing a paycheck; they are chasing their dreams. Champions are filled with hope while the "also-rans" are filled with excuses.

So what is so special about people who become wealthy? To learn this, you must *associate with successful people*. Association is powerful because it normalizes your experience of successful people and their accomplishments. That way, when you make your next million, you simply say "Of course!" We tend to fear what we don't know or understand. What you will realize is that people who make ten times what you make have idiosyncrasies, faults and blind spots. They also embody passion, confidence, vision and *belief*. You'll pick up little tidbits of wisdom sitting at the table of giants. You will become aware of the thoughts and behaviors of your own that do not align with your new associates. You will begin to see things through their eyes. You will transform your thinking!

One of the most empowering belief-building exercises that you can engage in is reading the stories of champions and thereby absorbing their beliefs. Learn about the challenges that other people have overcome and the massive victories they've enjoyed. You see, for every excuse that someone has, a successful person has faced an even more severe challenge and surmounted the obstacle. Consider the real-life examples in the following table.

Potential Excuse	Successful Person
I'm a dropout.	Michael Dell, founder of Dell Computers, became a billionaire at 32
I'm dyslexic.	Richard Branson, founder and CEO of the Virgin Group of companies
I have a hearing impairment.	Sylvester Stallone
I'm too short.	Tom Cruise
I have a speech impediment.	James Earl Jones
I'm too young.	Craig Kielburger, founder of Free the Children (at the age of 12)
I'm Afro-American.	Barack Obama
I'm blind and mute.	Helen Keller
No one has ever done this before!	The Wright Brothers
My teachers don't believe in me.	Fred Smith, founder of FedEx (was ridiculed by his college professors for his business concept of globally distributing packages)
I've been sexually abused.	Oprah Winfrey

So, what's your excuse?

Believe that You *Can* Do It

It is one thing to believe that another person can achieve success, it is quite another to visualize yourself as the one standing on the podium accepting the gold medal. Personal belief stems from several sources, including:

1. Past victories
2. Current self-image, through
    a. talents and abilities
    b. self-esteem
3. Future vision

Your self-image will establish the boundaries of your undertakings, and therefore all of your accomplishments. Lewis Timberlake, author of *Born to Win*, says, "Your self-image is your opinion of who you are divided by your opinion of what is takes to do the job. ... [I]t has nothing to do with your potential, but everything to do with your performance!" By mastering the strategies that fuel each of these areas, you will lay the foundation of a strong belief in yourself. Following are steps you can follow that will help you do this.

STEP 1: LIST YOUR 5 GREATEST VICTORIES

Remarkably, people have a strange habit of replaying negative memories in their mind over ... and over ... and over! What possible value does this offer? Aside from learning from the mistake in order to never repeat it again, this behavior serves no more value in life than stopping to stare at a car accident on the side of the road! The human fascination with disaster has always been a curiosity to me.

Think of your mind like the projector room in a movie theater. The projectionist is ever obedient: whatever movie you request, he'll play. And whatever movie you choose to play in your mind will powerfully shape your emotions. If you choose to play movies of your setbacks, embarrassments, defeats and moments of cowardice, how do you think you're going to feel? You are going to feel like an embarrassed, defeated coward. These emotions are not going to help you close any business deals or launch any new ventures. Instead, you need to fill your mind and spirit with feelings of courage, power, intensity, assuredness and conquest. So, which movies will convey these emotions? Your *victorious* movies!

Ask yourself: what are my proudest moments and accomplishments? Recall every race in school you've won, every test you got an A on, every sale you've ever closed and every goal you've ever checked off your list. You need to pull these memories out of storage and dust them off. Think about every challenge you've overcome, every setback you've rebounded from, every terror you've faced with courage, every defeat from which you have risen. Put your memory bank on "repeat loop" and play these images, day and night, in the future-shaping movie theater of your mind.

Take a moment and create a list of the Top 5 Greatest Victories you've ever accomplished. Maybe it was overcoming cancer. Maybe your parents didn't have money for groceries when you were a kid, and now you've bought them a new house. Maybe you are a black belt in karate. Maybe you closed a million dollars of sales this quarter. Maybe you have written and published your first book. Maybe you've raised a child in a loving and safe home, breaking the cycle of abuse from your past. Maybe you raised the most money for the United Way in your entire city this year. Maybe you scored the winning touchdown on your high-school football team ... or got drafted for the NFL! Maybe you took the prom queen home ... and stayed happily and successfully married all these years. Whatever your victories, take some time to bask in the glow of the incredible accomplishments you've achieved thus far in your life and enter the top five here:

My 5 Greatest Victories
1.
2.
3.
4.
5.

STEP 2: LIST YOUR 5 GREATEST ABILITIES

Having listed your victories of the past, now you'll want to take stock of the greatest personal qualities that shape your present. Each of us has talents and abilities that are special and unique. What are yours? Maybe you are highly organized, never missing a detail. Maybe you have a high level of energy and seem to get three days of work accomplished in one. Maybe you are charismatic and attract people to you like a magnet. Maybe you are empathetic and can read people's emotions. Perhaps you have an infectious sense of humor and make people feel happy in your presence. Maybe you are a great mediator, the person who soothes tensions between hostile groups or family members. Maybe you are a creative genius with music, words or food. Maybe you are spatially gifted and can design the layout and color scheme of a room to create a luxurious and comforting space. Maybe you are a born leader, and people follow you when you embark on a quest. Maybe you can connect seemingly disparate ideas effortlessly and create new possibilities that no one else ever conceived. Maybe you just flat out have guts, and you go after what you want. Whatever your talents and abilities, they are the tools in your toolbox that will help you to create your future prosperity. Honor your abilities by celebrating them and their value. Take a moment and consider, what are your five greatest abilities?

My 5 Greatest Abilities
1.
2.
3.
4.
5.

STEP 3: BUILD YOUR SELF-ESTEEM

To hold something in esteem means to have a high opinion of, or to value, it. Thus, *self*-esteem is, quite literally, how much you esteem or like yourself; the value that you feel you have as a person. Do you think that a person of low value can and will accomplish their goals? Not easily, if at all. If you hold yourself in low esteem, if you don't value yourself or you think poorly of yourself, you have little if any chance of getting what you desire. It's a simple concept to understand and a great deal of work to correct. But it is so important to your financial success, not to mention your relationships, health and personal sense of fulfillment. Self-esteem is a critical component in your path toward greatness.

It is always good policy to focus on your strengths. You want to find evidence to *refute your negative beliefs about yourself.* Do you find yourself saying "I'm clumsy" or "I'm foolish" or "Who would want to be with me?" You would find that language appalling if it came from a friend, so why would you accept it from yourself? For every negative belief you need to find evidence to blow it away. Ask yourself, "How am I attractive?" "How am I organized?" "How am I a leader?" Look for evidence to support these questions. When someone pays you a compliment, do you disregard it and focus instead on the negative? When you have an example of doing something right, do you overlook it and choose to remember only the screw-ups? Do you choose to hang around people who put you down and remind you of your failures? Successful people don't. To help you strengthen your self-esteem, complete the following statements:

I am a good person because:
I am a good spouse because:
I am a good parent because:
I am a good employee because:
I am a good boss because:
I am a good friend because:
I am a good neighbor because:
I am a good sibling because:
Strangers like me because:
I know I'm hardworking because:
I know I'm trustworthy because:
I know I'm caring because:
I know I'm fair because:
I know I'm worthy of love because:
I know I'm respectful because:
I deserve to be wealthy because:

Consider developing a *daily affirmation* statement to this effect. Just as you should create a statement affirming your future net worth, you should also create an affirmative statement of your future self-worth. You may choose to wake up each morning, smile and say, "I am grateful for the miracle of this day of my life. I am a smart, successful, passionate person who cares for and protects her family, and I can't wait to meet the other exceptional people who will join me in life's adventure today!"

Finally, you need to know that you will maintain these high qualities as you interact with people.

STEP 4: SHAPE YOUR VISION

Our subconscious mind can't tell the difference between what is real and what is imagined. This can have devastating effects if we allow our subconscious to make us fearful. Note the many social phobias that plague many Americans and how irrational they can seem to anyone who is not afflicted: fear of public speaking, fear of flying, fear of confined spaces, fear of open spaces, fear of germs, fear of spiders, and so on. People actually imagine that they are in mortal danger and act as if it were true! However, the flip side of the coin is also true: whatever *good* things you imagine, your subconscious will accept they are real, and you will act accordingly. With focused action toward attaining success, you will manifest your goals in real life. To do this, we must take conscious control over the programming of our subconscious mind.

There's a psychological technique called "autosuggestion" that was developed in the early twentieth century by apothecary Émile Coué. Napoleon Hill uses the term to describe the process of programming your subconscious mind in order to create your future. In his timeless classic *Think and Grow Rich*, Hill outlines six key steps on how to believe yourself into a million dollars. He goes on to say that these steps do not require hard work or specialized training in school. However, they do require a significant amount of *imagination*, as you must visualize the future in advance. As well, you must do so with a high level of emotion, as you have to be passionate about your personal quest in order to accomplish it.

The six steps that Hill describes are:

1. Decide *exactly* how much money you want. You can't just say "I want to be rich"; you need to specify an amount.
2. Decide what value or service you plan to offer. How hard are you willing to work and sacrifice? What are you willing to learn? Are there any limits on what you are willing to do in order to accomplish your goal? List these.
3. What is the deadline for accomplishing your goal? Don't say, "Next year," because that is a floating deadline and will always be 365 days away! Say, instead, something like, "By January 1, I will accomplish my goal of …".
4. Create a specific plan to accomplish your goal and take massive, immediate action executing your plan.
5. Create an emphatic "affirmation statement" of your goal. For example, "I will earn $1 million by January 1. I will do this through purchasing rental properties. I will take a course on commercial real estate, read voraciously on the topic, examine at least twenty investment properties per month and make my first offer in four weeks."
6. Read your affirmation out loud every morning when you wake up and every night when you go to bed. Your subconscious is the most open to programming at these times; for instance, you may wake up to your smartphone playing a certain song and you keep thinking about that song all day long. Read the statement with passion and visualize yourself having achieved the goal. Create a burning desire inside yourself for claiming your victory.

This is the formula that Napoleon Hill proclaims is one of the keys to success as used by Thomas Edison, Henry Ford, Andrew Carnegie and all the giants of industry at the turn of the twentieth century. Ask anyone who has ever achieved greatly, and they will all say that they'd seen it vividly in their imagination before their dream became true. Walt Disney had passed away by the time Disney World was expanding and Epcot Center was being built. When a reporter said to Disney's son, "It's a shame Walt wasn't around to see this," his son smiled and said, "He saw this before anyone else." To dismiss these ideas as silly would be at the peril of your goals. To adopt these strategies is to have the key to the treasure chest of opportunity for your future.

Your Financial Thermostat

How much money do you believe you deserve to make? This can be a challenging question for people to face. "*Deserve* to make?" they ask. "Why, I guess whatever my employer is willing to pay me!" In fact, most people don't even understand the power of the question in terms of how it drives all their decisions. But the truth in life is that we rise or fall based upon how we see ourselves, and most people simply don't see themselves as a millionaire in the making. In order to become wealthy, you must bolster your financial self-esteem and believe not only that you are worthy of the work involved, but that you are worthy of the reward.

Your monetary self-esteem is regulated by your "financial thermostat." This is a mental picture in your mind of not what you *can* make, not what you *will* make, but how much you think you *should* make. And you only ever make as much as you think you should. Make a little less, and you'll push hard to catch up. Make a little more, and you will subconsciously self-sabotage and find a way to blow your cash.

What is a financial thermostat and how does it work? Well, consider the thermostat in your home. You set the device to provide the ideal temperature. When the thermostat notices it is too cool, it will turn on the furnace to warm up your house; when it notices it is too warm, it will turn off the furnace and activate the air conditioner to cool it down. Whether it is hot or cold, your thermostat is a highly obedient mechanical servant and will ensure that you return to your most comfortable temperature.

A financial thermostat operates in a similar way, except that the device you program is your brain and the number you type into the device is the number of dollars you believe you should have in your bank account. Whatever number you put into the financial thermostat, it is also a highly obedient servant and it will work to push you toward achieving your goal.

If you grew up in an impoverished neighborhood where no one went to university and half the kids in your school ended up in jail, you may never have met anyone who makes a six-figure income. In fact, it probably seems like a fantasy to do anything other than menial work that will barely allow you to scrape by. Your thermostat is set so low it is unlikely that you will aspire to anything greater.

Now think from the perspective of someone from a middle-class family. If everyone you know makes $50,000 a year, you would probably relate to that figure and believe it is normal and natural to make $50,000. If you get laid off and find a new job making $35,000, you will feel some psychological tension. This is called "cognitive dissonance" in the language of cognitive behavioral therapy (CBT). The image you have of *where you are* does not align with the image of *where you should be*. You feel tension pushing you to improve things; you believe that life should be better. So you will keep looking for a better opportunity.

If you were raised in a family of multi-millionaire business owners, you probably believe that it is right and natural to own a business and make a seven-figure income. If you aren't doing so, you might feel that you are shooting a little low for your capabilities.

But here is where things get really interesting: your financial thermostat also has a *maximum* setting! This means that if you make *too* much money, you will feel cognitive dissonance as well. You'll actually feel awful being rich! This is commonly observed when people win the lottery. For many, winning $10 million is one of the most stressful experiences of their lives. First of all, they can't believe it really happened. Secondly, they don't picture themselves as millionaires. They have no idea how to carry themselves or handle the money. It all seems a little surreal. So the happy winners go on a spending spree. They blow the cash on vacations, cars and homes, and every fad business idea that comes their way. Quickly, everyone wants to be their friend. Second cousins to whom they haven't spoken in years start coming out of the woodwork and everyone wants a loan. People treat them like a bank and get angry if the lottery winners don't share their good fortune. So what happens? Within a few short years, the lottery winners are dead broke, back to where they started—if they are lucky.

What happened? What happened is that they never truly saw themselves as millionaires; they never really believed they deserved to make that much money. And so, their financial thermostat kicked in and began to burn their monetary mansion to the ground.

So, what's your financial thermostat set at? How much money do you honestly believe you deserve to make? However you answer this question, understand this: you'll never make any more, and if you do it will be a temporary aberration. Remember the adage: if all you ask of life is a penny, that's all you'll ever get. Consider the question again, and fill in the blanks below.

How much money do you honestly believe you deserve?
I deserve to make $ _____ per year.
I deserve to have $ _____ in savings.

Now consider this: how much would you *like* to make? How much would you like to have in savings ... and in net worth? I ask these questions after you've stipulated how much you deserve to make because people can become excited about their goals and have a false sense of bravado when speaking about them.

One of the critical components in defining what you want to make is not the desire to acquire wealth, but the simple belief that it is possible. Without belief, the embers of hope will not be nursed into a roaring fire of possibility and achievement. You will be timid in your actions and pessimistic in your goals. In order to become wealthy, you must genuinely *believe* you can! Thus, the way you reset your financial thermostat is by *building belief.*

Your Financial Lexicon

Words are the doorway to your mind. The words you choose are a reflection of your thoughts and beliefs. Because your mind is the fountainhead of wealth, the language that you choose to use to describe money is a key indicator in how prosperous your thoughts really are. *So, what language do you use to describe your relationship with money?*

Pay attention the next time someone is speaking about money and you will realize that the words they choose are either propelling them toward prosperity or condemning them to a life of want. How do they describe the wealthy families in their community? Do they say that those people are "lucky" or "greedy" or "they take advantage of people?" Don't expect money to be flowing toward anyone with these defeatist attitudes.

Words convey attitudes about wealth. Do your words empower you to see and believe in prosperity, or are they disempowering you and sapping you of energy and confidence? When you see someone drive by in a luxury car, do you crack a joke at their expense, saying, "Maybe he's compensating for something," or do you nod approvingly and say, "Wow! That person must be incredibly talented at what they do. Someday I will create enough wealth to enjoy that lifestyle!" Can you see how your words condemn you or free you? However you describe another person is really an autobiographical statement and you are describing the prosperity or poverty that your future holds! You are really describing what you think of yourself with the words you choose to use. Positive statements indicate that you picture yourself as a talented, capable, industrious, focused person; a task-finisher, someone with integrity, someone who is committed to excellence, someone who is on the path to massive riches.

Here are some examples of the difference between the "Language of Poverty" versus the "Language of Wealth." Which statements are most closely aligned with your own thinking?

The Language of POVERTY	The Language of WEALTH
There is a limited supply of money.	There is an abundant supply of money.
My boss won't give me a raise.	I'll raise more venture capital.
I pay my taxes first.	I deduct my expenses first, then pay tax.
Find a good company to work for.	Find a good company to buy.
Money doesn't grow on trees.	My ideas create money.
I don't have the money.	How can I raise the money?
I earn this much in salary.	I have this much in net worth.
My company pension will take care of me.	My rental income will take care of me.
I'll pay using credit.	I'll pay with cash.
It's on sale, so I'm saving money.	I purchase according to my plan.
You make money when you sell.	You make money when you buy.
I can never seem to get ahead.	I can create more wealth any time I desire.

continued

The Language of POVERTY	The Language of WEALTH
I deserve a new car.	I'll reward myself with a new car when I earn enough money in commissions.
My company is getting sold and I'm losing my house.	I'm selling my company and buying a new mansion.

The Law of Attraction

Make the decision that you will claim a massive financial victory, and you will direct your energies and attention upon this goal. It may seem almost magical to the layman who is unaware of these principles that you have engaged a very powerful truth: whatever you think about repeatedly, you will attract into your life. Some years ago, Rhonda Byrne's book *The Secret* reminded people of this truth and created renewed interest and awareness in how this universal mechanism works. To those not versed in the principles of attraction, there are four very important ones related to success. They are:

1. Magnetism
2. Reticular activating system (RAS)
3. Other people will join you in your quest
4. Personal motivation

Magnetism has to do with the fact that our thoughts are, quite literally, physical things. Our brain transmits electrical impulses as we think, and these impulses carry the information throughout our body for automatic and directed bodily function. However, when we become fixated on a goal and imbue our thoughts with massive emotion and passion, combined with daily repetition, the universe seems attuned to the patterns of energy that our brain transmits. Your thoughts can literally attract into your life the things, people and events that you focus on.

Reticular activating system (RAS) refers to a part of the brain that decides which information to pay attention to and which information to delete. Every day we are inundated with billions of bits of sensory data: visual, auditory, kinesthetic, olfactory and gustatory. In order to make sense of it all, our RAS has to take most of the incoming data and file it under "G" for garbage. It's impossible for most human beings to wade through the morass of data, and so most of the time you simply don't pay attention to what's going on around you; most people aren't present in the moment because of this.

Consider a simple example: you have just purchased a new car. As you drive down the street, you begin to notice the same make and model all around you! In fact, you are shocked to see "your" car at least a dozen times that morning. What happened? Did people suddenly find out that you got a new car and, because you are the driving force behind the consumer trends in your city, everyone decided to copy you the next day? Hardly. All the other cars were always on the road; it's just that it wasn't important to your brain to notice them. As soon as you purchased your car, you told your RAS that this information was significant. And thus, it began to notice what was in front of you all the time.

How does this apply to success? Well, there will literally be dozens of opportunities to generate wealth every day, but unless you've attuned your mind to them, you won't notice them and success will slip through your fingers. A friend may mention off-handedly, "I've just met with a brilliant tax attorney who's showing me how to use charitable donations to maximize my deductions." If you aren't focused on wealth, you might reply by saying, "That's nice." If you are focused on growing your net worth, you will likely stop the conversation and say, "Really? Tell me all about it."

The third principle is that other people will join you in your quest. If you are totally focused on attracting wealth into your life, you'll never be more than a few minutes away from talking to others about your dreams. Every cocktail party, every business networking event, every time you're in line getting coffee or groceries, your mind is focused on your quest. When people ask you how your day is going, you can't help but answer with enthusiasm. You're another day closer to achieving your dreams! People always want to jump on the bandwagon when they see someone going places; it's exhilarating! Invariably when they hear about the projects you are assembling, people will say, "What a coincidence! I've got a friend/sister/ colleague with whom you should connect. She's exactly the person you need for this!" Almost magically, doors open, connections are made and opportunities present themselves.

Lastly, you will attract success into your life simply because you are motivated to take action. A key principle in the law of attraction is that merely thinking about a goal is not enough; you must pursue it with vigor! Simply wanting to take someone to the dance is not enough; you must gather your courage and ask. Simply wanting to win a contract is not enough; you must create a compelling argument as to why you deserve to. Simply hoping that money arrives in your lap is futile; the intensity of your actions must match the grandeur of your dreams. You're going to accomplish what you set your mind to because it consumes you with such fervor that you can't bear to sit idle when there is one more phone call to make, one more proposal to develop, one more sale to close.

The Empowering Beliefs of the Wealthy

Why aren't more people rich? While it might be popular to say, "I didn't get the breaks the other guy did," the simple fact of the matter is that people who make it in life understand that *success needs no explanation, and failure allows no alibi.* Whatever you think about most, you will attract into your life; whatever future image you hold in your mind you will become. Consider the title of Napoleon Hill's *Think and Grow Rich*. Observe that it is not titled "Complain and Grow Rich" or "Lie Around and Grow Rich."

People who are truly rich simply think differently about money and success. Their subconscious mind is attuned to opportunity. Their confidence breaks down barriers that would paralyze lesser men. Their energy compels them to work through the night when fatigue has eroded the chest-thumping bravado of their competitors. Their vision allows them to see themselves standing in the future, clearly having accomplished their mission. By studying and mastering the thoughts of millionaires, you will create powerful possibilities for success in your life! Consider the following thoughts that will orient you for success:

- I must take *total responsibility* for my life.
- Luck is where preparation meets opportunity.
- I will create my own "mastermind team." (See Shift 5, Part III: Building Your Mastermind Team.)
- Whatever the mind of man can conceive and believe, it can achieve.
- If you help enough people get what they want, you get what you want.
- Wealth is generated through creativity.
- "Materialism" is where your paycheck stops.
- Healthy parents want their kids to succeed.
- It's better that good people have the money.
- Money helps alleviate suffering.
- I deserve it.
- I am good enough.
- I can do it!

The Limiting Beliefs of the Poor

In stark contrast, the thought patterns of people who do not succeed are unsurprisingly dismal. Filled with complaints, excuses and guilt-ridden fears, the people who fail will always look to external circumstances, never inward. They don't realize that their negative thinking has hobbled them in the Olympic sprint toward their fiscal finish line.

Do you harbor any negative beliefs about money or wealthy people? Consider how you would complete these sentences:

Rich people got that way by:
Being rich means that I must:
When I see a wealthy person, I think:
If I had a lot of money, people would:

Your responses above will provide insight into what some of your money beliefs might be. If any beliefs are negative, they will undoubtedly stand in the way of your aspirations. What follows is a comprehensive explanation of the most common money-losing beliefs. Honestly consider if any of these wealth-eroding beliefs have burrowed their way into your mind. It's important to recognize if any of these beliefs are harbored within you; if so, it will be critical to your success that you root out and eradicate them.

Money can't buy happiness

It is true that no store or website offers a product labeled "happiness." In fact, happiness is created within us, by us. However, saying money can't buy happiness is as illogical as saying that money can't buy gravity or sunlight. Nor can money currently buy a new cerebral cortex (although that may change in time). The fact that money can't buy some things of value does not invalidate the many other things it can buy. Happiness is the expression of values, and while money in and of itself is not a value, its possession is valuable. What money will do is alleviate suffering caused by financial pressures. Money will fix a flat tire, a leaky roof or a leaky heart valve. Money will take away the stress of not making your mortgage payment. Anyone who says that money can't buy happiness should tell that to the impoverished university graduate who has thousands of dollars in student loans, or to the child awaiting a $250,000 surgery or to the family needing cash to escape a war-torn genocidal nightmare.

Only lucky people get rich

This is nonsense. Ask anyone who quit their job in order to start working for themselves if they are "lucky." Ask any entrepreneur who had to mortgage his house to make payroll if he is "lucky" when the business finally flourishes. Ask Colonel Harland Sanders, founder of Kentucky Fried Chicken, if he was lucky at the age of 65 with no pension, living in his car, being rejected 1,008 times as he tried to sell his chicken recipe … and yet he tried one more time and finally made the sale. Luck was not the deciding factor in his success: grit and persistence were. Oprah Winfrey famously says, "Luck is where preparation and opportunity meet." To ascribe the concept of luck to the success of any entrepreneur is to take a position that your life is determined not by you, but by fate; and that if you have no control over your destiny then it really isn't your fault if you don't succeed. This is a cop-out and an utterly crippling belief system to hold.

I'm from the wrong family

This belief is similar to the notion of luck in that you believe wealth is a result of being a winner in the "lottery of the womb." Without question it can be advantageous to have parents with the material resources to fund your projects, the connections to open doors and help you assemble a winning team, and the mindset of million-aire thinking, which they can teach you at the kitchen table growing up. Bill Gates famously got into business with IBM because his mother, a high-ranking executive at IBM, opened the door for him. But for every Bill Gates, there is a George Soros whose parents barely escaped war-ravaged Europe with the shirts on their backs. Your parents' position in life is a starting point but never the determining factor for your success. In fact, having a wealthy family may prove detrimental to your future success. We can agree that there are and have always been examples of trust-fund babies whose billionaire parents throw cash at them rather than doing the tough work of actually being around to parent them and instill proper values. If you ever feel jealous of the opulent life of kids whose parents seem to give them all the resources, open all the doors and hand them the golden keys to the castle, replace this feeling of envy with that of pity. Without the struggle required to build character, handing someone money rarely results in wealth creation.

I don't want to take advantage of people

Is it possible to become very wealthy by taking advantage of people? Absolutely, yes. Is it the only way to become wealthy? Absolutely not. For every swindler there is a savior, and you have the power to decide which of these you will be. Zig Ziglar, motivational speaker and author, says, "Help enough people get what they want and you will get what you want." Consider that if you are honest in describing your product and service, then every transaction is a moral one. You are offering something that will enhance the quality of life for someone else and accepting money in exchange.

It's wrong to be materialistic

The simple fact of the matter is that *everyone* is materialistic. It is physically impossible to live on the earth without being materialistic. Food, clothing and shelter are material. As soon as you engage in eating anything, wearing anything or living anywhere, you are automatically materialistic. "But wait!" people say. "I didn't mean *me*! I meant my co-worker whose car is nicer than mine! *He* is materialistic!" When you press people who purport to be anti-materialistic to define what they mean, they will simply offer sneering generalizations of the opulent lifestyle of the rich and famous ... or the guy next door who has a bigger flatscreen TV than they do. You see, anyone who complains about materialism is actually referring only to people who make more money than *them*.

People won't like me if I'm rich

You will always attract quality people into your life by being a person of quality. Showing respect to others and being appreciative of and interested in them are the cornerstones to relating well. Any significant change in life usually causes you to relate less to those who have not grown along with you. When you get married, your single friends relate less. When you have a child, your childless friends have less in common than the new friends you've met who are starting families. It is possible that some people won't like you if you become wealthy. However, nothing significant was ever accomplished in the annals of history by trying to make everyone like you.

I don't want to "show up" my parents

This comes from an irrational notion of what it means to be respectful to your parents. If making more money than your father would embarrass him, causing him to become cross with you and want to cut you out of his life, then this is an issue for him and his therapist. It should have zero impact on you. If someone has an irrational, illogical belief system, you should never feel obliged to pander to it. Imagine the type of world it would be if no one became more successful than their parents. There would only be two choices left: reach the same level of success, or have even less success. It would only take a few generations with this mindset to end up penniless in the streets. Any parent who holds this negative view and plants seeds of guilt in their children for aspiring toward achievement should be ashamed.

I don't want to be greedy

Michael Douglas won an Oscar for Best Actor in the movie *Wall Street*, primarily because of his famous monologue "Greed is good." Greed creates opportunity where there is none; it creates jobs, products and services to consume, and a healthy economy. The failure and subsequent collapse of communism almost worldwide is an overwhelming argument against any doctrine that does not encourage people to achieve and succeed. Greed need not be only reserved for money: people are greedy for love, for health and safety, and for a feeling of purpose and meaning in their lives. So when you say "greedy," what do you mean? Usually you mean "having more than someone else." What is immoral about that? If you work harder than someone else, why would you not deserve more money? Nobody wins if nobody tries. You should always be greedy for experiencing the greatest life possible, and you should be proud of it.

I don't want to sacrifice my health and my marriage

There is no point in becoming wealthy at the cost of your health and marriage. I don't support that way of living and I don't encourage you to sacrifice either of these extremely valuable things. But why would you believe that this is the cost of becoming wealthy? Have you met someone who is wealthy who did it at the cost of these fundamental values? If so, they are not a good role model and I don't encourage you to follow their example. Making time for nutrition, proper sleep and exercise is one of the keys of being wealthy. If you're lying flat out on your back in the hospital because you've failed to make your health a priority, you're going to stop watching your business and money will slip through your fingers. If you neg-lect your marriage and come home to an empty house with your spouse's closet empty and the kids gone, are you going to be able to do that important business presentation tomorrow? Of course not! Wealth is a means of creating *more* health and *greater* relation-ships; its pursuit should never be a cancer that erodes the most im-portant things in your life.

Action Steps

Your mind holds the combination that can unlock the vault to great prosperity, or it can seal the treasure away from your physical reach. It falls to you to take control of your thoughts and direct them toward prosperity. You must believe that you are a person of value; you must focus on your greatest strengths and abilities; you must see yourself earning more money than you have imagined before.

Build belief in yourself by reviewing your top five greatest strengths and abilities. What do you do right? What is your unique specialty? What is the genius that makes you special? Why are you a good person?

Reset your financial thermostat to attract and allow greater prosperity into your life. How much do you truly believe you deserve to make? How much would you like to make?

Words have power: you must choose language that is affirming and attracts the reality that you aspire to. Monitor yourself over the next few days and weeks and audit any language that describes negative outcomes. Speak only of what you want to attract.

Adopt the beliefs of successful millionaires, and erase the negative beliefs of poverty thinking.

In the next chapter we will examine the relationship between four qualities of "being" and "wealth" with these foci: integrity, intentionality, impeccability and invincibility.

ACT ON THE PRINCIPLES OF WEALTH FOLLOWERSHIP

When attempting to create wealth, most people take an approach that focuses on taking certain steps — the *how* to become rich. This is an understandable error and easily correctable. The truth is that in order to have what wealthy people have, you must do what wealthy people do. And, in order for that to occur, you must become what wealthy people are.

Whenever I present this concept to those who are struggling to attract greater riches, I am always amused that they do not recognize this fundamental truth. I might field these types of questions instead:

- Where should I purchase real estate?
- What business should I start or invest in?
- What innovations should I fund?
- Should I diversify my portfolio or focus on a few key investments?
- How is wealth grown and sustained?

My answer to these questions is that the *how* is much less important than the *who*.

Who you are in your being—at your core—is at the center of my message to you. Far more important than the hot stock tip or a lesson on no-money-down real estate, this concept will revolutionize your life if you are open to it and allow yourself to consider it. The nature of your spirit, your essence, is the magnet that will attract wealth or conversely work against you.

German professor, author and philosopher Martin Heidegger referred to it as "being in the world." In his book *Existence and Being* he writes:

> *The concept of being is the most universal one, as was also realized by Aristotle, Thomas and Hegel, and its universality goes beyond any genius. "[B]eing" cannot be comprehended as anything that is. It cannot be deduced from any higher concepts and it cannot be presented by any lower ones. "Being" is not something like a stone, a plant, a table, a man … "[B]eing" seems somehow an evident concept.*

"Being" as a concept is ineffable, but within the scope of this book I can offer insights on who you are being in the world and how this directly influences your success, peace of mind and level of satisfaction.

We are always in touch with the world of "being," though we are not always conscious of it. It's just like breathing: we breathe to survive, yet we rarely consciously think of breathing. What people do is physical evidence of their being. How they conduct themselves is their calling card to the rest of the world.

What qualities shape our being? I believe our attitude, personality and behavior synergistically define who we are. Add to this our fundamental points of view in life. We all see life through our own stained-glass window; our points of view are based on our experiences and our upbringing, and the result is a built-in value system or moral code.

Maxwell Maltz, author of *Psycho-Cybernetics*, refers to this as "self-image." Dr. Carl Rogers, author of numerous books in the realm of humanistic psychology, refers to it as "self-concept" or "self-structure." Cognitive behavioral therapy calls these our "core beliefs." To use my earlier metaphor, the colors in our stained-glass window shape our view of the world and create who we are being in the world.

So, how do you perceive the world? Is it fair or unfair? Friendly or dangerous? Is your career or business life made up of pleasant experiences or is it onerous and filled with disappointments?

Our world view has a direct impact on everyone in our lives, including our clients and business partners. If you see the world as untrustworthy, you'll probably doubt much of what people tell you. If you view the world as a friendly place, you're more likely to trust people. No matter how you try to disguise your inner self, your core radiates from inside. In any given moment throughout the day, you will doubt or trust your clients and partners based on your fundamental points of view of the world. In other words, if you view the world as dangerous, you're probably a cautious and doubtful entrepreneur. Regardless of how you try to appear, you are always *being* how you feel.

You Control the Rules

In the movie *The Matrix*, the protagonist Neo receives advice from his mentor, Morpheus. Morpheus explains that Neo will be able to fight and defeat his enemies in the computer-simulated world of the Matrix. Why? Because his enemies' actions are based on mathematical rules and laws of physics, and because of that they will never be as strong or as fast as Neo. Neo's abilities in the Matrix are based only on his mind, his imagination. Neo is free from the rules that constrain his opponents. He is free to create and shape the world to his will, so his eventual victory is assured.

In our world, wealth is created by our minds. And wealthy people reject the "rules" that constrain those who are not wealthy, such as:

- It takes money to make money.
- I don't have the experience.
- I'm not good enough.
- Who am I to believe that I can be rich?
- This deal is too big for me.

Wealthy people understand, like Neo, that they create their own rules and bend their reality to suit their will.

Notice, by the way, that the "rules" that hinder or expand the creation of wealth are largely self-created. That is, you have to agree to them in order for them to be true for you. So why are you agreeing to limiting rules? Why did you wake up one day and agree to any of the "rules" that I've listed above, or to any others that are lurking in the sewers of your negative subconscious beliefs? In order for these "rules" to be true, you must first give them power by accepting them, and this is a power that you have the ability to revoke at any instant.

In the coming pages, I am going to discuss the critical components of being a wealthy person. You must cast aside your belief in any limiting notions and embrace the following values:

1. Integrity
2. Intentionality
3. Impeccability
4. Invincibility

INTEGRITY: "MORAL SOUNDNESS; COMPLETENESS"

Do You Want to Be Right, or Rich?

The common understanding of integrity is the concept of doing the right thing, behaving in a fair and just way, honoring your word and keeping your promises. In the structural sense, integrity means that all parts of a building or body are aligned and function properly; that they are an indivisible whole; that they are healthy, strong and free from weakness.

We know that in order to have money, you do not have to have integrity. It's true: you need look no further than criminal activity to realize you can rob a widow of her handbag and have the cash you've desired. In fact, you don't even need to be that extreme. You could short the stocks in your own company and squeeze your partner out of the deal, seizing ownership of your firm when your partner sells his shares at bargain-basement prices. Indeed, why even be as dramatic as that? You might give up your integrity by simply doing some business under the table with your company's top clients. The money goes into your pocket and not the firm's, but who's going to know or care?

While it is obvious that there are countless examples of millionaires who don't have integrity, it might seem counterintuitive at this point to postulate that you should always have integrity. But I'm going to say it very clearly: to live a sustainable life of the highest quality, you need to have integrity. Why? Because in order to get rich and stay that way, you have to be a certain way. Let's consider some examples.

Observe what becomes of the mafia lord who blazes a trail of violence to secure his wealth, or the city official who accepts bribes under the table, or the thug on the street who knocks over a convenience store, or the salesman who lies about the mileage on his expense report. What becomes of these people over the long term? Here is a clue to the answer: whoever you are being is going to come through pretty consistently in every area of your life.

So, follow the trail. The salesman who lies about his mileage to his boss is going to lie to his kids about why he missed their football game — and they'll lose respect for him because they can tell when Dad isn't owning up. The thug on the street who collects his money through intimidation is cavorting with other people who believe the way to get things is to take them ... and right now his "friends" are eyeing the cash in his pocket and getting ready to jump him in the alley. The city official who will lie to his constituents about the true nature of his loyalty will lie to his wife about the suspicious photographs that have gone viral ... and she's gone past the point of discussion; she's already packing her suitcases. The mafia kingpin who has climbed his way to the top of the mountain by blazing a trail of violence will find that violence finds its way to his front door ... and this time what comes through the door is a shotgun blast. Do any of these scenarios seem appealing to you? I should hope not. What's the point of being rich if you lose respect, love and physical well-being?

Whoever you are being it is absolutely true you may cheat the system and get away with it for a moment — but not forever. If you've obtained money from people by swindling them, just remember that everything in life comes full circle. And karma is a patient, mystical force. It waits, it watches, and it returns to you whatever you put out into the universe.

So, here are some fundamentals to being a person with integrity:

Don't do the wrong thing. If the other stock brokers are trading with inside information, avoid them and avoid the practice. If the partners in your consulting firm are over-billing clients for the work done, don't follow suit. If you are part of a consortium that is buying property from an elderly couple who do not know the true value of their property, and will be cheated, don't be a part of it.

Do the right thing. It's not enough to stand by and not have the filth of corruption splash onto you; you need to step up and stamp it out. Don't stand by idly when you see injustice; get involved and stand up for people who deserve the assistance. If you find out your CEO has sold stock and not reported it to the SEC, you need to decide what your values are. If your company has just asked you to cook the financial books and they are willing to pay you $50,000 to never speak about it in court, you need to decide what a clean conscience is worth to you. If you have made a mistake and a partner is taking the blame, it's not enough to just defend their innocence, you must also admit your fault. If someone else has made a mistake that you have allowed, you must take responsibility for it.

Keep your promises. Your handshake should be as good as any legal document. Your word is your worth, and your worth is your word. A lot of people misunderstand the parameters of how and when to keep promises, but really, it's quite simple: keep promises — always. This means that when it is inconvenient, you keep your promise. If it costs you unexpected time, you keep your promise. If it costs you money, you keep your promise. Why such a strict standard? So that whenever you consider making a promise, you do so very cautiously. When you have resolved that you will always keep your promises, no matter what, you will not make promises idly or without thoughtful consideration of their full impact on your life. You may find that you actually end up not making as many promises, because you are fully aware that even if it becomes a hassle to you, you'll still need to follow through and do what you say. But when you do make a promise, everyone around you knows that it is as good as done. Do you understand how transformational that quality is in business? Being certain — 100 percent — that when a person says they will be at a certain place, at a certain time, having completed certain work, or bringing a certain amount of money, they will do so —well, it becomes enjoyable to do business with them. It is freeing. It feels effortless.

If you knew how to be rich, you'd already be there. What we can surmise from this is that you don't yet know how to be rich. Stop taking your own advice and start listening to an expert. If you want to keep getting the same results you've always gotten, just keep whispering words of sage counsel into your own ear.

The need to be "right" and make someone else "wrong" is such a compelling necessity for many people. People will actually choose to lose money in order to keep their old bad habits and emotional baggage and make a point against an adversary. Ego trumps profit for such a person. Perhaps winning an argument is a way of increasing their low self-worth. Perhaps they are being competitive or argumentative, or maybe they simply have an angry and combative spirit. The need to fight overrides their need for wealth. Which one is the bigger driver for you? If a millionaire says something that absolutely contradicts your belief system but is advice that would make you a small fortune, how do you react? Do you need to prove why the millionaire is wrong just so you can save face? Do you have to make him or her wrong so you can feel right?

Your ego can be a major stumbling block on your road to wealth. For some people, admitting that they don't have all the answers can be very humbling. In fact, it might even be embarrassing to admit temporary defeat and ask for help. But if you have the courage to seek mentorship from someone wise, massively successful and willing to offer their wisdom … take it. Humble yourself and sit at the foot of a true master. Glean every morsel of wisdom that you can.

INTENTIONALITY: "DONE ON PURPOSE"

Own Where You Are

If you want to be wealthy, you need to rid yourself of any self-deluding justifications, rationalizations or excuses. You have to understand this fundamental truth: your net worth is a direct result of every decision you've made up to this point. And all of your decisions are a product of your thinking.

You can't go through life expecting to be rich while simultaneously playing the blame game. Pointing the finger at your teachers, your parents or your boss creates nothing more than a story about why you didn't make it. And whenever you point the finger at someone else, just remember you've got three fingers pointing right back at you.

Take total responsibility for everything that has been manifested in your life. Do you realize the power in doing this? It is so liberating to simply say, "I am in control of my life." It means that whatever you've created, you can undo. If you are the source of your reality, if you are truly the creator of your current results, then you are the creator of your future.

You have the power to rewrite your thinking and remake your actions in an instant. If you have been pessimistic, you can choose to fill yourself with resolve. If you have been filled with self-doubt, you can see all of your strengths and greatness. If you have yearned for success yet hesitated too long, you can set your sights on future opportunity and strike while the iron is hot. You can create new businesses, break open new markets, double your revenue, attract new relationships and strengthen existing ones. All of this is within reach when you take total and absolute responsibility for your life.

Get Off the Wrong Bus

Are you pretending to be something you're not? Are you wearing a façade of confidence that serves as a thin veneer to your self-doubt?

Do you intellectually accept the tenets described in the first chapter on the "millionaire mindset," but emotionally you experience a sense of tension between your thoughts and your feelings?

Many people fail at becoming wealthy because deep down they receive some value in financial struggle. Maybe you've been telling yourself a story all these years that the reason you're not getting the results in your career that you want is because someone else is holding you back. Maybe you tell a story to yourself that you didn't close the sale because you don't really deserve to win. Maybe your parents weren't as loving as you wish they had been, and those hurts and disappointments have become a convenient excuse to explain away all your missed opportunities and failed attempts at success. And maybe you get a huge payoff from telling these stories.

An accepted view of insanity is doing the same thing over and over and expecting a different result. Many people try a new way of getting rich without first learning a new way of being; therefore they get the same miserable results. A simple comparison would be romantic relationships. So many people go from one failed relationship to the next, thinking that if they just pick the right person, then they will finally enjoy bliss. They wonder, "How do I keep attracting the same terrible partner, over and over?" What they fail to understand is that even though their partners keep changing, they themselves stay the same! They remain needy, abrupt, controlling, complaining, confrontational or conflict-avoidant. And until they change, they will continue to attract the same type of person. A person must first be responsible for where they are now in order to open the doorway to transformation.

Werner Erhard is the founder of Erhard Seminars Training (often referred to as est) and an inspiration in the education I embody; his works lies at the core of my teachings. Erhard shares a powerful analogy about the need for radical personal change. He says that many people are traveling through life on a proverbial bus. They don't like where they are headed, so they get up and change seats on the bus. They congratulate themselves on making such a bold move, making a stand and taking action to create change in their life! However, they are still on the bus, and it is heading in the same direction. Nothing has fundamentally changed.

In order for you to be wealthy, you've got to get off your bus. What is this bus? It is you, the person you are being. It is your beliefs, your attitudes, your actions, your spirit ... not just your actions, not just your mind, but the deepest essence of who you are as a person. Until you change your true nature, your circumstances will deliver you to the same deserted bus stop. When who you are being changes in the necessary ways, you will begin to attract success.

For example, for a person to have the wealth that a successful business owner has, they must do what the business owner has done — that is, build a successful business. To launch their own business, they must do the action of leaving their job. But in order to leave their job, they must be courageous. What that looks like is making decisions and choices that are fueled by accountability, bravery and commitment.

You could review a hundred different business proposals, but if you fundamentally believe that you are going to fail, then you will find a reason to say no to every one of them! If an opportunity to bring a new product into the country presents itself, but you just don't have the hunger and drive to start a business from scratch, your product will never find a market and flourish. You have to *be* ambitious. You have to *be* driven. You have to *be* a visionary. Being transcends doing, which is the seedling of having.

To attract prosperity, don't just change seats, trying a new action without changing your character and mindset. Get off the wrong bus!

IMPECCABILITY: "WITHOUT A FAULT OR FLAW"

Pursue with Purpose

Excellence is a function of consistency in spite of circumstances. Excellence is a commitment to maintaining the highest caliber of being, the strictest discipline to high performance, and a focus on never-ending improvement. Excellence becomes a measuring stick against which our very nature is measured.

To be impeccable means that our conduct, our performance, our thoughts, our environment and the final product that we deliver to the world has passed a rigorous battery of examinations. The constant standard that we hold ourselves to is this: could I improve? Have I spent myself wholly in the worthy pursuit of my ideals? Can I honestly say that I have given my all to this endeavor, or deep down do I know that I held back? Was I truly committed to winning with integrity?

It's not about being perfect or having achieved the pinnacle of human potential. It is possible to have areas of your life that are not impeccable. However, *pursue with purpose*. What this means is to examine where your commitment is. You could have a relationship that is not working as well as you would like it to, but be in full communication with your partner around that idea. If your commitment is to making it work, then your energy and focus is in achieving an "impeccable" relationship. Perfect is never achieved. It's strived for, always remaining out of reach, so that you are forever reaching.

Following are some specific ways in which you can endeavor to be impeccable and thereby manifest this value in your life.

Use impeccable language. Your words are a clear advertisement of your thinking. Callous, hurtful or venomous words are the canary in the coal mine for everyone who crosses your path; people can see pretty quickly that your spirit is an angry or negative one and will want to avoid you.

At every opportunity, uplift people. Compliment people. Point out what they did right. Point out what you like best about them. It is good mental discipline to look for the good in all things and all people, and articulating it out loud forces you to follow through with the discipline. People hear enough negativity in their lives: you can be a beacon of positivity in their world. Uplift people and you will be more attractive to them.

Enjoy the inner peace of an impeccable mind and spirit. Keeping a clear conscience is enormously rewarding. It is so freeing to follow your inner voice and do what you know is the right thing to do.

When you violate your word, you have to worry about that person getting back at you. When you lie, you have to worry about remembering the details of your story. When you break your own values, you have to worry about being found out. When you break the law, you have to worry about jail time.

But when you honor your word, you have the peace of knowing that you are building trust. When you are honest, you have the priceless value of integrity as your greatest asset. When you honor your values, you are living in a congruent way and all the pieces of your life fit together perfectly. And when you honor the law, you know that the law can be your ardent defender against injustice.

Have an impeccable record. Life accumulates. The small actions we take and words that we speak create reactions and results, epic in size or seemingly insignificant. But each action, positive or negative, is like a deposit or withdrawal from a bank account of good will and public image. Controversies abound of politicians and public servants who grow a false sense of omnipotence, believing they are above the rules. They feel all-powerful and believe they can cheat on their taxes, their constituents or their spouse.

In the realm of creating money, invariably we are offering to make someone's life better in exchange for their money. We might be selling a product to clients, helping our partners raise venture capital or purchasing a property from a seller on terms and pricing that are agreeable to both parties. In all business dealings we are forming a relationship, albeit sometimes only momentary and transactional. But if we swindle our clients, if we double-cross those partners, if we defraud the people we deal with, two things will happen. First, those people will never trust us again, and so we will never do business with them again. Second, they will tell everyone in sight, and we'll have lost that potential business as well.

When people trust you, when they trust that you will do the right thing, they are more apt to trust their hard-earned cash in your hands. When the word on the street is that you are out to con the next sucker, people will treat you like a leper. Be impeccable in your dealings with people and your public record will read like advertising copy to attract a wave of enthusiastic investors and partners.

Maintain an impeccable environment. First impressions are formed in an instant. The way you dress is your statement to the world about your view of yourself. It is an unfortunate reality that many people make an impression based solely on how a person looks, but it is pragmatic to recognize this reality and conduct ourselves accordingly. How do you see yourself, and how best can you convey that image to the world in an instant? Do you see yourself as capable, proactive, organized, successful and meticulous, with an attention to detail? If so, let the world know.

When clients visit your office, or friends and family visit your home, what sort of environment are they walking into? Just as your clothes are a way of showing the world who you are *being* in an instant, your physical environment has the same effect. Whether it is your house, desk or car, are you an orderly and tidy person? Do all things have their place? Are you disciplined and meticulous? Knowing that business is a team sport and you need to attract people to work with and people to sell to, is your environment pleasant and welcoming to your partners and clients?

If you want to make a leap forward in personal accountability, resolve that you will hold yourself to the highest standards of cleanliness, tidiness and organization, and watch as these qualities manifest themselves in your business dealings. Notice that when you are excellent in this area, you have a sense of control and power over your life. A small personal victory in this area is a powerful asset on your path to success.

Extol impeccable customer service. If you are to attract great wealth in your ventures, you must value the people you deal with. If you have sold a product, the transaction doesn't end when the cash is in your account. The greatest business leaders are ultimately the greatest servants of those with whom they deal, and it needs to be one of your highest pleasures to ensure that your customers are not just satisfied with your service, they are amazed by it.

What could you do today to amaze your customers? What level of service is your competition unwilling to offer? When you outperform your competitors, you will take delight in wooing their patrons away. What extra way can you make the customer experience memorable, so that your customers tell their friends and family? What follow-up skills can you employ to touch base with your clients after their purchase to ensure their satisfaction?

Take care of the small details. Take inventory of all the financial gaps, incomplete business and dealings that you must take care of. Take action. Close the gaps and bring your records up to date. Organizational skills are fundamental in wealth creation. If you are giving financial advice, your own books need to be in order. If you have received mail, it must be opened and correspondence must be replied to. If a voicemail is left, you must return the call. If a client has asked a question, you must get back to them with a prompt and accurate answer. If a meeting is set, you must be on time, prepared and focused. If a vendor has submitted an invoice, you must pay them in a timely manner. If today is payday, you must make payroll for your staff even if it means forgoing your salary and getting a bank loan. When you submit a report, it must be double-checked for spelling and grammatical errors. Dot your i's and cross your t's. Your numbers must all be triple-checked for accuracy. Every piece of work that you complete must bear your signature of excellence. Don't do things "well enough"; do them to perfection.

INVINCIBILITY: "THAT WHICH CANNOT BE CONQUERED OR OVERCOME"

When Your Confidence Is Deeper than Your Pockets

To be wealthy, you must be invincible. It is not enough to conceive of a grand scheme and pursue treasure, to woo fortune, to attract customers and invite riches into your life. Anything magnificent seems somehow to attract a magnificent obstacle. The nature of the universe is such that the moment we begin to draw our plans and take a bold step forward, we are assailed with unexpected drama. Opponents that we could not have imagined rise up to deny our easy passage to the land of milk and honey. And because of this, we must be greater than the obstacles we face.

Donald Trump is an excellent example of someone who is *being* invincible. Trump made headlines in the late 1980s for his stupendous real estate deals in New York and blazed a trail of success for himself. However, in the early 1990s he was overextended and his creditors began to call in his debts. His empire seemingly dashed, hanging on by a financial thread, Trump had to fight off the creditors to keep his doors open. It looked like he had suffered unrecoverable losses to his real estate empire. But Trump would never settle for failure. It wouldn't matter if you took away his fame and connections and left him penniless in the street. He could walk into any boardroom and through sheer charisma command a meeting with the CEO. His intelligence, persistence and unwavering confidence in himself make Donald Trump an invincible titan in the markets he does business in.

What would you do if you were wiped out financially? I can tell you that in the early 2000s I lost an amount in the high six-figures in the stock market crash. But who I am as a person is what creates my wealth, and like many successful business people I simply reapplied the core principles of wealth creation that built my net worth in the first place, and I battled back to replace and grow my wealth since then.

I am blessed to have been coached by an extraordinary man, a former Navy SEAL. Through the gift of our time together, I have come to learn about the extreme experiences that soldiers like Jack are subjected to. Navy SEALs go through incredibly intense training, including SERE (Survival, Evasion, Resistance and Escape) School. The training culminates in being subjected to what might be described as torture at the hands of their trainers in order to prepare them mentally to deal with actual torture, should such a terrible situation occur. What is true about torture is this: everyone has a breaking point. Any human will reach a point where they can't take it anymore and they'll disclose or confess any information. My question to you is this: what is your mental breaking point? When you face a business setback, when would you throw in the towel?

What would it take to knock you down financially and keep you there? More important is this question: What would it take to break your spirit? Would it take your business partner cheating you out of money? Would it take your biggest customer switching over to your competitors? Would it take regulators shutting down your business unfairly? Would it take your top salesman stealing your business? Would it take your suppliers being weeks or months late on key shipments? Would it take the economy suffering incredible setbacks and driving business out of the country? Would it take war, disaster, tragedy, recession, disloyalty, theft or persecution? What truly would need to happen for you to say, "I can't do it" or "I'm not strong enough to handle this"?

Your confidence is a much greater asset than your wallet. The market valuation of your net worth might be a fixed number today, whereas the market value of your self-assurance might speak of incalculable wealth.

Action Steps

You have seen how the quality of your character truly shines through in every moment. People are attuned to who you are *being* and can see through a façade of pretense. In order to live the greatest life possible, you must *be* the greatest version of yourself. In order to have success, you must *be* "success." Get very clear on who and what you are *being* and you will open doors previously thought to be impassable.

1. **INTEGRITY:** Remember that not doing the wrong thing is different from doing the right thing. Inaction in a situation where moral courage is required does not make you a courageous person. You must remember to stand up and do the right thing, even when it costs you in the short term. Over the long term, integrity will attract quality people and exceptional opportunity into your life.

2. **INTENTIONALITY:** Changing seats on your bus won't take you in a different direction. You have to get clear about the rules of the game you are playing, and choose to play the game you set out to play, rather than the one that other people create for you.

3. **IMPECCABILITY:** *Being* committed to excellence is the hallmark of a champion. How can you raise your standards in the various areas of your life? How can you raise the standard to which you hold yourself in the realm of your personal space, your body, your relationships, your service to clients and your treatment of people?

4. **INVINCIBILITY:** *Being* a courageous person yields courageous actions. In what way can you show more courage? Is there an area of your life where you have failed to show courage and you know you must make amends for it? Is there a situation approaching in your life that calls for courage? How can you prepare for this situation?

Having focused on the concepts of being and wealth in this chapter, we turn next to a discussion of destiny and how to shape your vision for the possible.

DESIGN YOUR DESTINY

What exactly do you want? What does it look like? What will it take to acquire, maintain and share those things that are integral to your destiny with others? Once you make that choice, decide with definitiveness.

The Internet, the mapping of DNA, the Space Shuttle, cell phones, planes, cars, radio, and the printing press—all of these creations of humankind were first creations of human *imagination*. To a person without vision, a rough-hewn hunk of marble is a rock; to a visionary like Michelangelo, it is a masterpiece waiting to be revealed. When he first laid eyes on the marble that would become one of his most celebrated accomplishments, the statue of David, the master said, "I *saw* the angel in the marble and I carved until I set him free."

The men and women who lay claim to their destiny see through obstacles to the possibilities beyond. It is not enough to simply *wish* for something; it is not enough to simply *hope* for something. The giants of history desired things that they focused on with such intensity as to render their potent thoughts indistinguishable from physical facts. They willed their riches into existence with the power of their focus and belief. They vividly saw things not as they *are* but as they *would be*, and it worked.

Bill Gates says that Microsoft was founded on the vision of there one day being a computer on every desk and in every home. Similarly, Henry Ford once envisioned a car for every man. Thomas Edison dreamed—and nighttime darkness disappeared. All great men and women begin with their goal firmly etched in their mind, every nuance and detail alive with color and texture. They harness the full power of their subconscious and make their dreams so realistic that their subconscious mind cannot tell between fact and fiction. They have a clear vision for their future.

It Begins with a Vision

On August 28, 1963, a crowd of over 200,000 civil rights supporters met at the foot of the Lincoln Memorial to hear the words of one of the greatest visionaries of all time. In his historic "I Have a Dream" speech, Martin Luther King, Jr., took the microphone and spoke in great detail about the vision he had for the future: how one day little black boys and girls would play with little white boys and girls, and that his children would not be judged by the color of their skin but by the content of their character.

Consider the power of King's words. He described how he desired to see the future. He described what will happen in the future he saw. He described how people will treat each other. He described how in every place we would "let freedom ring." He infused his description with passion and energy. It is a masterpiece of visionary composition and oration.

Now, consider the ripple that King's words created that day in the Civil Rights Movement of the sixties. Forty-five years later, to the day, after the "I Have a Dream" speech, Barack Obama took the stage at the Democratic National Convention as the first black presidential nominee in the United States.

Whether your politics are conservative or liberal, and regardless of your assessment of Obama's presidency, you can't help but be struck by the transformation in American society that has brought forth the election of a black man to the highest office in the country. It is a momentous accomplishment and a testament to the power of Martin Luther King, Jr.

The reasons for developing your vision are seemingly boundless and clearly compelling, but here are just a few to consider. Having a clear vision:

- gives you a feeling of certainty about your future
- helps you to make decisions quickly
- creates a long-term focus
- generates energy and vitality
- attracts like-minded people to you
- makes you resilient to setbacks and discouragement
- reveals resources and opportunities you never saw before
- allows you to create the future you desire
- gives you a greater sense of purpose
- forces you to address your personal shortcomings, and
- allows you to become the greatest version of yourself.

Let us consider progressing from a clear vision to a powerful vision. A powerful vision:

1. is commanding in scale
2. is detail-rich
3. requires boldness
4. is precise
5. requires personal growth
6. aligns with your values
7. fuels you with energy
8. attracts followers
9. invites obstacles, and
10. leads to triumph.

Now let's take a few moments together to consider each of these in detail.

1. A POWERFUL VISION IS COMMANDING IN SCALE

Think of an extremely successful man or woman whom you admire. Now, attempt to picture a person having acquired such greatness by thinking small thoughts and taking minuscule actions, being barely shielded by a thin veneer of confidence. It is a futile exercise because *no such person exists*. The man or woman who has captured your admiration in truth thinks *colossal* thoughts, took *massive* action and has a bulletproof *shield* of confidence to defend them. Everything about them is larger than life—particularly their thoughts.

You must be the same. You must envision grandeur, opulence and luxury engulfing you. If your financial thermostat says you are worth only $100,000 a year, then you must shatter your self-imposed glass ceiling. You must see yourself competing for business, quoting twice the price of your competitors, with your customers hungrily thirsting for your services regardless. You must see your enterprise stretching into new territories, new continents. You must envision your factory needing to add a midnight shift to keep up with the overwhelming demand for your creation. You must see your IPO causing an explosion of activity on the trading floor as the value of your stock swiftly ascends. You must see all things greater, larger, faster, broader—reaching heights only yet imagined!

2. A POWERFUL VISION IS DETAIL-RICH

For your subconscious to fully buy into the imagined reality you are creating, you must make the images in your mind so vibrant, so colorful, that you cannot help but believe you are experiencing them in the present. The picture in your mind's eye must be drenched with realism. You have to engage all of your senses to bring your future world to life.

Because we experience life through our five senses, we can experience our future using the same formula. The average person will imagine their future as a distant blurry scene, with monochrome colors and tinny sound. Their goals will be vague and amorphous. There will be a fog of uncertainty surrounding all that they expect to see and experience.

Contrast that with the vision you will have. Your vision must be bright with vibrant color and sharply contrasted images with clearly defined lines. The movement of the people in your vision is purposeful, powerful and certain. The sound of your voice is clear and confident. You see yourself doing exactly what you want, accomplishing exactly what you must. In a boardroom, you feel the polished wood of the oak table on which you rest your hands. In front of stockholders, your voice echoes with confidence throughout the auditorium as you wield your microphone like Excalibur. On the golf course, you delight in the manicured grounds, the swing of the club as your body traces a perfect arc, the sounds of your new business partners cheering as your ball settles perfectly in the cup. At dinner, the clinking of wine glasses and the aroma of your delicious meal surround you as you celebrate your new merger.

In all instances, no detail of your exceptional future is left to chance. You see yourself gliding expertly up to your dock in your 50-foot yacht. You feel the exhilaration as your Porsche accelerates through a curve. You see the smile of a child in a cancer ward that your philanthropy has helped establish. You have left no detail to chance, because your future success is not a game of chance. You have taken control and crystallized your vision in vibrant detail.

3. A POWERFUL VISION REQUIRES BOLDNESS

The exceptional life is not for the faint of heart. The great rewards are not left to those meek and timid souls who fear the threat of defeat, nor is treasure unearthed by those who tire quickly from the effort. No, the playing field of life is for the bold and strong. The timid fill the bleachers while the real champions take their place along the scrimmage line below. Life is an emotional full-contact sport, and visionaries don their psychological armor for the contest they have joined.

It was boldness that inspired Christopher Columbus to set sail across the Atlantic in search of India, toward the edge of the flat earth. It was boldness that first gave Copernicus and later Galileo the courage to tell the world — at the threat of death — that the earth revolved around the sun. It was boldness that compelled a black Jackie Robinson to dare step up to the bat on the white Brooklyn Dodgers baseball team, knowing the hostility he would face.

A vision is not a memory of what *was* or a picture of what *is* — it is a dream of what *will be*. And because what you have envisioned does not yet exist, you must have the courage to tempt fate and overcome pessimism, doubt and fatigue. It takes courage to pursue what you believe to be right, particularly when the gap between the present and the future seems so large. It takes persistence to continue putting one foot in front of the other on your journey, without loss of enthusiasm.

4. A POWERFUL VISION IS PRECISE

Since he was four years old, Tiger Woods has had a singular goal: to be *the greatest golfer of all time.* He did not envision himself to be "merely" highly talented, nor does he desire to be *one* of the best or even the very best *today.* Woods has willed himself to become the greatest golfer of all time. He has a list of Jack Nicklaus' career accomplishments on his wall and takes massive pleasure in breaking the records previously set by "The Golden Bear," personally checking off one accomplishment after another. Tiger Woods knows exactly what he wants. He is now being eyed as the first sports figure that will be able to earn $1 billion from earnings *alone,* not including product endorsements.

Do you doubt him? I don't. It is what he lives, sleeps, eats and breathes. Does your vision consume you in the same way? Can you describe exactly what you want? Putting your goals down on paper will help you to do this. The act of putting pen to paper forces your mind to specify your dream. A written statement is concrete; it carries weight in your mind because we assign greater value to written contracts.

No architect would sign off on blueprints until every measurement had been recorded and confirmed. No builder would even begin removing dirt with a bulldozer until the blueprints had been verified; they would be paralyzed with uncertainty. Likewise, you will bounce randomly from one opportunity to the next like a pinball, forever hoping to land on your true path to success, until you get clear on exactly what you want and how you can get it. A properly crafted vision invites execution because its precise image engenders a feeling of confidence, a feeling that *this* is the correct path to take.

5. A POWERFUL VISION REQUIRES PERSONAL GROWTH

Your vision is a picture of what your world can become. And all progress in our external experience is born of the progress we have generated first within our internal experience. It's about making the decision and *choosing* to be courageous, concise, specific, daring and authentic—choosing a way of being that moves, touches and empowers you to take on your vision with a vengeance. The act of *becoming* is about the end result of measurable difference: like becoming healthy, wealthy or happy. It's the net result of having lived life *being* healthy, wealthy or happy *first* in your mind. What type of person must you become in order to reach your destiny? Are there any defects of character that are holding you back from creating the life you desire? All successful people are willing to hold a mirror up to their character and look deeply into who and what they truly are.

If there are skeletons in your closet, if there is deception and malice in your spirit, if you aren't a strong enough person to finish what you start, then all the dreaming in the world will be for naught. If you are fearful, you must become courageous. If you lack knowledge, you must become studious. If you are harsh, you must become compassionate. If you are weak, you must become powerful. You must become the person you see in your vision. Your personal growth holds the key to your success.

A powerful example of personal growth is seen in Theodore Roosevelt. One of the most celebrated presidents in American history, Roosevelt was noteworthy for, among many things, his peak physical condition. He took judo, climbed mountains, swam rivers and even created a volunteer group of cowboys called the "Rough Riders," whom he led bravely into battle in the Spanish–American War. When he was police commissioner of New York City, he woke early in the day to walk the beat with other officers, just to see that they were at work. He was a model of health and vigor. But this was not always the case!

When he was a boy, young Theodore was sickly and asthmatic. He was bullied at school and was in no condition to fight back. His father, a wealthy and powerful businessman, admonished Teddy and explained that his mind could only accomplish what his body allowed; that with a weak body, he would get weak results. He instructed Teddy to toughen up his body through regular and intense exercise: swimming, rowing and calisthenics. To combat the bullies, the boy also began taking boxing lessons.

Roosevelt's rigorous physical discipline created energy and power in him that would serve him well throughout his life of great accomplishments. Your rigorous discipline toward self-improvement, in whatever way that requires your personal focus, will allow you to do the same!

Your personal growth is a choice. It will result from the powerful experience of having chosen the path *to grow* every day. Just like

working out every day as you promised yourself, it matters less what you eventually look like; it's what it does for you each day that counts.

6. A POWERFUL VISION ALIGNS WITH YOUR VALUES

One cannot hold two contradictory thoughts in the conscious mind simultaneously. You cannot believe that "All things come to those who wait" while also thinking "He who hesitates is lost." Similarly, one cannot profess to hold a vision of the world they dream of if that vision violates their deepest and most treasured beliefs and values.

To be completely congruent and maintain your personal integrity, the vision you pursue must align with your principles. To ignore this is to tempt disaster, for a man who works feverishly against the very things he truly loves will ensure his defeat through self-sabotage. You cannot help but shoot yourself down if subconsciously what you think you are doing is wrong.

Therefore, careful attention must be paid in the creation and pursuit of your vision. Consider what happens when champions begin to ignore their own inner voice. Tony Robbins, celebrated peak performance coach—who is a friend and mentor of mine, and who I have had the chance to work with and tour alongside—shares a personal example in his own story. He speaks often of the rapid success he enjoyed at the age of 19 and the rapid downfall he suffered by the age of 24. The cause? He began to self-sabotage, believing that he wasn't deserving of the money because of his friends' materialistic disapproval. So he treated people roughly, was late for key meetings and guaranteed his infant company's swift destruction. Despite a powerful vision that he had long held of serving and training people, his incongruent belief system caused his temporary defeat.

With values that are congruent with your greater vision, you won't suffer any internal conflict; your course will be pure and straight, and your aim will find its mark.

7. A POWERFUL VISION FUELS YOU WITH ENERGY

People consumed with their vision do not complain of insomnia. There is never a day where they find themselves drowsily lying in bed, staring at the ceiling and wondering how to "kill some time." People with a vision are compelled to take action, to drive themselves toward the attainment of their ideals, and they possess a boundless energy that their less-motivated counterparts can't comprehend. "How do you have the vigor to carry on at this late hour?" their friends and family ask. Those people don't understand the inspiring nature of a true dream. When you see that your dreams are about to come true, you may be too excited to sleep.

You'll know when you are gripped tightly by your true vision: you'll be so excited you won't succumb to fatigue. Your mind will be brimming with ideas, marketing strategies, product designs, financial transactions, people to meet and agreements to secure. The visionary within you will struggle with quieting the enthusiastic voices in your mind.

8. A POWERFUL VISION ATTRACTS FOLLOWERS

Like attracts like. Your compelling vision will not only invigorate you, it will draw people toward you who wish to share in your journey. People can sense when the person they are speaking with has their mental engine in "park" or in "fifth gear." People want to get on the bandwagon and join those who are going places. This is to your advantage, as most major accomplishments require a small army of people, and *all* of them require the assistance of mentors and supporters.

When he was 12 years old, a young boy from Richmond Hill, Ontario, named Craig Kielburger happened to read a story in his local newspaper about another boy, also 12, across the world in Asia. The boy had been speaking out against child labor, having worked in a labor camp himself until his rescue, and the article explained that this young boy had been assassinated because of his outspoken stance. Craig was shocked. He felt he needed to do something immediately. He went to the library and researched everything he could about child labor. He saw a day where these children would be free from the abuse of the labor camps and given a chance for a better life.

The next day in school, Craig asked his teacher if he could do a presentation to the students. The teacher agreed, and Craig shared the newspaper article he had read, how outraged he felt and his belief that the children must be freed. He looked at the faces in his class and stated, "I'm going to start a charity organization to free the children. Who is with me???" A dozen kids put their hands in the air, providing Craig with a team willing to follow his vision. Today, Craig has partnered with Oprah Winfrey and built more than 650 schools around the world for disadvantaged children. He has a massive organization of volunteer and youth workers, with tens of thousands of high school students around North America donating time and energy toward fundraising activities. Craig has a huge following, because people are attracted to his vision.

9. A POWERFUL VISION INVITES OBSTACLES

It may seem ironic that the moment you resolve to achieve a goal, the universe seemingly conspires to trip you up. On these days it might feel that you're facing a frustrating mathematical equation: the greater the goal involved, the more challenging the obstacle that threatens your journey. Don't be discouraged, and don't be surprised when you face a few setbacks. Remember this and let it be a comfort to you in those times: if the challenges you face seem nearly insurmountable, you are most assuredly heading in the right direction.

A goal that is easily achieved is then easily achievable by almost anyone, so what is the value inherent in such a goal? Scarcity creates value, and difficulties foster scarcity. You wouldn't feel nearly as proud of owning a 100-foot yacht if every slouch you knew had one parked out back as well. You've got one, unlike your neighbors, because you were willing to endure setbacks and hardships that they were not.

Most people are scared away from their future because, to paraphrase Henry Ford, when opportunity comes knocking, it's dressed in overalls and looks like work. People won't see the nights you are working without sleep, or the times you're getting a bank loan to make payroll that Friday—they only see the result after the hard work is done, and they call it "luck." You weren't lucky. Overcoming obstacles is simply part of the story for history's greatest victories.

10. A POWERFUL VISION LEADS TO TRIUMPH

In May 1992, Canadian rowing champion Silken Laumann was training for that year's Summer Olympics when her boat was struck by the boat of a competing German team. Her leg was smashed, muscle cleaved and bone clearly visible. This was less than *three months* before the Olympics. Everyone told her that they would understand if she were to quit. Except Laumann wasn't a quitter. After intensive surgery, she was back in the water by June, and at the Olympics she rowed into the history books by earning a bronze medal. Consider this example whenever you're facing challenges as you pursue your vision—you are following in some remarkable footsteps!

Define Your Ultimate Mission

In order to live a fulfilling life of purpose, you must first define what your mission in life is. Far too many men and women toil away in pursuit of a goal, only to finally accomplish the goal and realize that it was never what they wanted for themselves in the first place. So, before we pursue a dream we must truly define the dream that we want to achieve.

Success can be measured in different ways, and the way that you define the finish line will have an impact on which race you choose to run. For example, if you define success as net worth or the amount of money that you accumulate, your focus and energy will be directed to increasing the size of your bank account. But if you choose to define success as *life worth*, your impact on the world can be even greater—and manifest greater material wealth as a byproduct.

What is life worth? *Internal life worth* denotes all the intangibles that make life worth living: health, happiness, integrity, relationships and so on. Your definition will be highly personal and subjective, based upon your value system. *External life worth* can be measured by the positive impact you have on the world around you, the number of lives that you touch and make better because of your work and your presence. Is the world a better place because you are in it? This is the question answered by external life worth.

It is a tragedy of life that many people sacrifice the irreplaceable years of their lives in the pursuit of money, before considering the pursuit of meaning. Mother Teresa and Mahatma Gandhi are examples of people who did the opposite; they invested the years of their lives with great focus on positively impacting the lives of others, without thought of material gain—and the world speaks of their names and their lives with reverence because of their contribution.

So, what might your ultimate purpose be? If you could do something truly magnificent with your life to make the world a better place, what would you do? How could you improve the lives of the people whom you touch? These are deeply personal questions. But one of the greatest joys of the human experience is having the opportunity to consider questions like these, then answering them and pursuing your mission with vigor. Allow me to suggest some questions that will prompt your creativity and help you clarify a greater purpose in your life:

- If you could accomplish anything, what would it be?
- What do you want your life to stand for?
- How do you want to be remembered?
- What good could your wealth be used for?
- What do you feel would give your life greater purpose?
- What cause in the world stirs your heart?
- Is there a way to ensure your life is geared toward the things that really matter to you in the long run?
- What mission do you want to accomplish?

Be creative as you ponder these questions and capture your thoughts on paper, filling in the following:

As I look past my immediate goals of today, I feel I have a larger goal to accomplish before the end of my life. The great mission that I feel my life is meant for is:

Something that I could do today to take even a small step forward in my mission is:

As time passes, one way that I could invest more time, energy, attention or resources in my mission is to:

There are several key people who can have a massive impact in my journey to complete my ultimate life mission, and so they must be made aware of my mission and perhaps enrolled in it. These people are:

> If I am truly going to accomplish my ultimate mission, I absolutely must make the following investment in my mission:
>
> If I had an additional $10,000 to invest toward achieving my mission, the best thing to do with that money would be:

Your Destiny Checklist

As we've discussed, in order to create the future you want, the priorities you visualize must be supported by your goals. This raises the questions: What *are* your deepest priorities? What is your highest concern? What do you value the most? Defining what matters most requires you to identify your non-negotiables—the things on which you are not willing to compromise.

However you choose to answer this question, your actions yield results that have consequences, either good or bad. Whatever we care about most, we invest time in. Whatever we nurture will flourish, and whatever we leave untended will perish. If we value relationships, we will make time for family. If we value honesty, we will admit mistakes. If we value wealth, we will start our own business. But how greatly do you value your priorities? For if you value friendship over honesty, you may avoid hurting a friend's feelings but lose the opportunity to offer constructive criticism; and if you value wealth over relationships, your kids will have access to their trust fund but perhaps not to you.

If you forced yourself to define your priorities, what would you say they are? I'm going to invite you to take the next few minutes and engage in this very revealing exercise. What's the purpose in doing this? Sometimes we try to attain the right *priority* through the wrong *goal*. For example, we might have a priority of wanting our kids to love us, so we work late into the evening to achieve the goal of earning money for their education, while perhaps all they really want is our time and attention. Without clarifying our priorities, we may end up spending time pursuing empty goals when the real goal was available to us all along.

Below I offer a list of possible priorities that you may value in your life. This list is by no means exhaustive, and you can of course add other priorities to the list. What I'd like you to do is check off the five most important values in your life. Afterward, I'd like you to take a second pass at reviewing the list, but this time with an eye toward what top five priorities you believe you are actually living today. For example, if you feel that you value a specific charity but it doesn't get any of your time, energy or attention, then it may not be included in the second list. So, if you had to select your top five priorities, what would they be?

☐ Money
☐ Independence
☐ Community
☐ Deepening relationships with people I love
☐ My health
☐ Adventure
☐ Starting a business
☐ A specific charity or cause
☐ Meeting new people
☐ Volunteer efforts
☐ Travel
☐ Education
☐ The arts

☐ Work
☐ Recreational pursuits
☐ Living ecologically
☐ Making a difference
☐ Faith
☐ Creativity
☐ Thoughtfulness
☐ Learning
☐ Fame
☐ Solitude
☐ Fun

Other:
☐ _____
☐ _____
☐ _____

Which of the priorities are the top five in terms of importance to you?
1.
2.
3.
4.
5.

Which of the priorities take up the most of your time, energy and attention?
1.
2.
3.
4.
5.

Now that you've identified your top five priorities and identified where your energy actually goes, take a moment to consider the following questions:

- What made you choose the priorities that you selected?
- What is the deeper meaning behind your choices?
- What core values are revealed in your choices?
- How do you manifest these priorities today?
- Why are there differences between what you say you want and what you actually create in your life?
- What percentage of time do your priorities actually get?
- What could you improve about yourself to truly attract these priorities into your life?
- What do you need to change in order to be aligned with your priorities? Who and what do you need to *be*?

It is important to clarify our priorities before we define our goals, because goals are usually a means to accomplish a priority, not the other way around. In his best-selling book *The 7 Habits of Highly Effective People*, Stephen Covey shares an analogy of the difference between managers with goals and leaders with priorities. While building a road through a jungle, the managers of the the group are focused on goals such as sharpening axes, holding tree-cutting seminars and clearing a certain number of square feet per hour. The leader's job is to climb the tree and make sure they are chopping down the trees in the right direction. When the leader realizes they are off track and their goals are not aligned with their priorities, he shouts down from the treetops, "Wrong direction in the jungle!" To this the managers (focused only on goals) shout back, "Shut up! We're making progress!" Knowing your priorities ensures that your goals are congruent with your values and that you can channel your energy for maximum success.

Designing Your Ultimate Future

For the next few moments, pretend that there are no limits. Allow your imagination to reveal your deepest desires and ultimate dreams. Become almost childlike again in your ability to ask the universe for what you truly want. Think of everything you want your ultimate future to contain: what does your financial situation look like, exactly? What does a luxurious life look life to you? What about your level of health and energy? Your relationships? How about your emotional health, your time for rest and relaxation, your desire for philanthropy and contribution? All of these areas are components in your ultimate future, and the more vividly you paint these images in your mind's eye, the more likely you are to attain them.

On the following pages, I provide a treasure chest of ideas to prompt your brainstorming. As you begin to create your list, be conscious of philanthropy, charity, goodwill and spirituality, as well as being green-conscious and good to the earth. Let these suggestions serve as a catalyst to tempt your mental palate so that you can taste the greatness your future can become!

Finances

- [ ] What would you like your annual income to be in one year? Five years? Ten?
- [ ] What would you like your net worth to be when you are 40? 50? 60?
- [ ] What assets would you like to acquire?
- [ ] What amount would you like to contribute to your children's education? What schools would you like to send them to? Ivy League universities? What would the yearly costs be?
- [ ] How much would you like to spend on vacations each year?
- [ ] What about a miscellaneous fund for new "toys?"
- [ ] How much liquid cash would you like to have for investments, available at any time for when opportunities arise?

- [ ] What type of investments have you always longed to make?
- [ ] How big would you like your retirement nest egg to be?
- [ ] How much money would you like to donate to charity every year? How about over your lifetime?
- [ ] How much money will you truly require to live the life of your dreams?

Take a moment and describe your desired financial situation:

Business & Career

- [ ] If you had unlimited money, what would you like to do?
- [ ] Is there a career you've always dreamed of?
- [ ] With more money, how could you market your existing business more effectively?
- [ ] What amount of sales would you like to generate this year?
- [ ] What new markets would you like to expand into?
- [ ] Are there new products or services you've dreamed of adding to your existing catalogue?
- [ ] What hot new trends are emerging that you would like to jump on? What trends would you like to create?
- [ ] Would you like to own real estate? What kind? Commercial properties, rental homes, apartment buildings, factories, landfills, power centers, undeveloped farm land, downtown office towers?

Residence

- ☐ Where would you like your primary residence to be situated? What city? What country?
- ☐ What type of residence is it? A penthouse, a luxury lodge, a country estate, a suburban mansion, a sprawling ranch with hundreds of acres, an ocean-front castle with a dock for your yacht?
- ☐ Would you like a second or third home? A vacation home in the tropics? A ski chalet in the Swiss Alps?
- ☐ Would you like a cottage on the lake?
- ☐ How large would you like your home to be? How many square feet? How many rooms? Bedrooms, bathrooms?
- ☐ How many people could you host for a party at your home at one time? What about a sit-down dinner in your great hall for 100 guests?
- ☐ What is the feeling you get when you walk into your home? Warmth, grandeur, exclusivity, luxury, family?
- ☐ What does the kitchen look like? Do you have a chef on your staff? Do you have a walk-in pantry? Marble countertops? A Sub-Zero commercial refrigerator?
- ☐ What about your master bedroom? What features make it your luxurious retreat? Does it have its own fireplace? Home theater? King-size bed? Canopy over the bed?

Armoire? Reading nook with relaxing chairs? Luxurious linens with the highest thread count? Walkout deck to view your grounds? Kitchenette to enjoy a late-night snack or early-morning coffee?

- [ ] What does your office look like? What type of desk do you have? Do you have a boardroom table for meetings with your employees or partners? A bank of monitors tuned to current developments in business from around the world? Art adorning the walls?

- [ ] Do you have a library? What books are there, and how many? A reading chair and fireplace?

- [ ] Do you have a games and entertainment room? Do you have a pool table? Darts? Mini-putt? Ping pong, air hockey or foosball table? Pinball machine? Video games projected on a wide-screen with four controllers for your friends? A bar complete with barstools and brass foot rail? Flat-screen TV to watch the game? Sports memorabilia?

- [ ] Home theater: how many can be seated? Are there wide, comfortable couches with drink holders? Surround sound and the latest theater technology? Do you have a "lobby" with a popcorn machine and movie posters adorning the walls? Ice cream freezer like they have at Baskin-Robbins? Candy dispenser?

- [ ] Staff: would you have a housekeeper? A chef? A groundskeeper and pool man? Someone to wash your cars? A security guard at the front gate? A personal assistant?

- [ ] What is your backyard like? Do you have a wood deck? Intricate stone work? A gazebo? A fire pit for roasting marshmallows and telling stories late at night? A massive chrome barbeque? A hot tub? Poolside chairs for tanning? Speakers to enjoy some great music?

- [ ] Does your backyard have pathways to walk? Trees to provide shade and natural beauty? Wrought-iron lamps to light the way? Small bridges to cross over your man-made river? A one-hole golf course to practice your swing? Riding trails for your mountain bike? A forest to play paintball war games?

Take a moment to describe your "castle of choice":

Vehicles

- [ ] What cars would you have parked in your garage? Lamborghini, Ferrari, Audi R8, Porsche, Mercedes-Benz, BMW, Rolls-Royce, Bentley, Hummer, Range Rover or a restored classic car? Maybe an Infiniti or a Lexus? A stretch limo? Would you take a Navigator and make a stretch limo out of it? A Mercedes-Maybach? What about a luxury office on wheels?
- [ ] Do you have a yacht?
- [ ] A luxury motor coach?
- [ ] A private jet?
- [ ] A helicopter?
- [ ] A Jet Ski?
- [ ] A custom motorcycle from *American Chopper*?
- [ ] A monster truck?

Take a moment to describe your "dream machines":

Happiness

- [ ] What makes you feel happy?
- [ ] What does "happiness" feel like to you? An adrenaline rush? A tranquil peace? Relaxation? Adventure?
- [ ] What will it take to get it?
- [ ] How will you know when you've gotten it?
- [ ] Do you enjoy hearing jokes? Sharing them? Would you like to share even more?
- [ ] What emotional states do you want to experience?
- [ ] Do you ever feel great for no reason?
- [ ] When you are feeling down, do you know how to pick yourself up?
- [ ] Do you tend to enjoy your day? What can you do to enjoy this moment, right now?
- [ ] Do you enjoy doing random acts of kindness? What could you do that would make someone feel really appreciated?
- [ ] Could you compliment people more often?

Travel

- ☐ What countries would you like to visit?
- ☐ What hotels have you dreamed of staying in?
- ☐ What foods and cultures have been at the top of your list to experience?
- ☐ How long would you like to go away for? A week? A month?
- ☐ How many times a year would you like to vacation? Once? Once a quarter?

Would you like to ...

- ☐ Take your kids to Walt Disney World ... then drive cross-country and visit Disneyland in California?
- ☐ Go on safari and photograph the lions, elephants and zebras in Kenya?
- ☐ Walk along the Great Wall of China?
- ☐ Visit the pyramids of Egypt?
- ☐ Tour the Colosseum in Rome?
- ☐ Visit the Mayan ruins in Mexico?
- ☐ Sail up the Amazon River?
- ☐ Visit the Forbidden City in China?

- ☐ What about the Taj Mahal in India?
- ☐ Spend a night at the ice hotel in Quebec City?
- ☐ Trek across the Arctic tundra?
- ☐ Have dinner at base camp of Mount Everest ...
- ☐ ... then plan your assault on the summit?
- ☐ Zip line through a rain forest canopy?
- ☐ Stay in the Burj Al Arab in Dubai, the world's first 7-star hotel?
- ☐ Stay in the Presidential Suite at the Atlantis Paradise Island resort in the Bahamas?
- ☐ Sit in the Parthenon of Athens, Greece?
- ☐ Rent a Caribbean island for a week with your friends?
- ☐ What about just buying the island permanently?

Take a moment to describe your ultimate vacation:

Health

- ☐ Do you have the typical strength and energy of someone your age? Someone younger? Someone older?
- ☐ Did your last physical examination return a positive report?
- ☐ Are you free of illness and disease?

- [ ] Do you have the body you want? If not, can you clearly visualize the body that you want?
- [ ] What sort of injuries and ailments would you like to eliminate from your daily experience?
- [ ] What improvements in your health would you like to enjoy?
- [ ] Would you like to increase your muscle mass and strength? By how much?
- [ ] Would you like to lose fat? What is your current body fat percentage and what would you like it to be?
- [ ] What would you like your measurements to be?
- [ ] Would you like to exercise more regularly? Would you like to work out with a friend? A fitness coach?
- [ ] Do you want to improve your diet? Do you eat foods that give you the nutrition and energy you need?
- [ ] Can you lift the weight you want?
- [ ] Can you run as far and as fast for as long as you want?
- [ ] What physical activities do you enjoy? Which activities have you stopped doing that you would like to start again? Which activities would you like to try?

Take a moment to describe your desired state of health:

Philanthropy

- [ ] Who is counting on you?
- [ ] How will the world benefit from your wealth?
- [ ] Who in your family would you like to help, and how? Would you pay off your parents' mortgage? Help send your nephew or niece to a prestigious university? Help pay your brother's medical bills?
- [ ] Who else other than you and your immediate family "wins" thanks to your help?
- [ ] What causes are important to you?
- [ ] What mission fuels your purpose? After you collect all the toys and go on all the vacations, what do you truly want to do with your life?
- [ ] Has anyone helped you in times of great need, and would you like to somehow repay the favor?
- [ ] How would you like to be remembered? To be eulogized?
- [ ] Is the world a better place because you were born?
- [ ] If there was one way you *could* make the world a better place, what would it be?
- [ ] How would you like to serve?
- [ ] Whom do you want to protect?
- [ ] What injustices enrage you? How will you fight back against those crimes?
- [ ] How would you like to serve the causes you believe in? Would you like to give money? Would you like to volunteer your time? What about offering resources or connections?
- [ ] Have you ever wanted to help with Habitat for Humanity?
- [ ] Volunteer at your local hospital, women's shelter, animal hospice?
- [ ] Hand out food and clothing to the homeless?
- [ ] Devote time to school kids through Young Achievers?
- [ ] Be a facilitator for Challenge Day?
- [ ] Teach life skills at the local prison?

- [ ] Help find jobs for people out of work?
- [ ] Offer training for immigrants?
- [ ] Build a school in a developing country through Free the Children?
- [ ] Give out medical supplies in Kenya through World Vision?
- [ ] Sponsor a child overseas?
- [ ] Send a child to college who has the grades ... but not the dollars?
- [ ] Become a foster parent and provide a safe home for kids?
- [ ] Adopt an orphaned or foster child?
- [ ] Donate money to global housing projects or respond to a charitable cause?

Take a moment to describe your greatest cause:

Personal Growth

- [ ] Have you ever thought of taking a night school course for the fun of the subject? Which courses interest you?
- [ ] Would you like to learn a new language?
- [ ] Improve your memory skills?
- [ ] Learn to master chess?
- [ ] Confront a fear that has plagued you and destroy the fear?

- [ ] Eliminate a personal trait that holds you back from success in business or in relationships?
- [ ] Adopt a quality of character that you feel you are lacking, perhaps becoming more patient, more forgiving, more proactive, more organized, more relaxed, more outgoing, more confident or more encouraging?
- [ ] Develop communication skills for presenting one-to-one, to a few or to many?

Take a moment to describe your desired personal growth:

Hobbies

- [ ] What do you do for fun? If you felt you had more time, what would you do? What did you used to do for fun before you got so busy, that you would like to start again?
- [ ] Would you like to learn a musical instrument? Piano, guitar, drums, violin, your own voice?
- [ ] Would you like to learn to dance? Salsa, jive, waltz, ballet or hip-hop breakdancing?
- [ ] Would you like to learn to ride a horse? Fly a plane? A helicopter?
- [ ] Would you like to write a book? A symphony? A play? A movie script?

- ☐ Would you like to act in your local community theater? Act in commercials? Be an extra on a movie set? Have a speaking part in a movie?
- ☐ Do you like photography? What camera would you like? Would you take still life, moving, black-and-white or color? Would you enter your photos in contests?
- ☐ Do you enjoy arts and crafts? Scrapbooking, crochet, knitting?
- ☐ Painting? Which painter is your inspiration?
- ☐ Home decoration?
- ☐ Gardening?
- ☐ Would you like to take a cooking class and surprise your friends and family?
- ☐ Would you like to try bungee jumping?
- ☐ What about hang gliding?
- ☐ Have you ever thought of skydiving?
- ☐ Scuba diving and seeing great shipwrecks in warm Caribbean waters?

Take a moment to describe your passionate pursuits:

Envision Tomorrow

Now I'd like to take you on a journey of visualization. Drawing from some of the potential goals you may have selected, I have crafted examples of visualizing these goals having been attained. As you read them, recognize the sensory detail that goes into a powerful vision. See yourself in these situations. Feel yourself having achieved this level of success.

The positive power of a clear vision cannot be understated. Napoleon Hill says, "The imagination is literally the workshop wherein are fashioned all plans created by man ... it has been said that man can create anything he can imagine." Follow me as we step into some examples of your possible future in the next few moments together. These examples will illustrate the scale and detail you will want to include as you create the vision tailored to your own desires. Sit back, relax and imagine ...

VISUALIZING WEALTH: YOUR "CASTLE OF CHOICE"

Imagine driving your dream car through the front gates of your ultimate dream home, the most opulent vision that your mind can see, your "castle of choice." Perhaps it is a manor home with servants and a coach house. It could be on a beach, on a mountain top or looking out at the waves of an ocean. It could be a penthouse overlooking a stunning cityscape.

Imagine it's a sunny day as you travel the tree-lined drive, while overhead the trees form a lush canopy. The pattern of light and shadows ripples along the smooth hood of your car. Sunlight is winking off the hood. Your car door is opened for you. Walking up the steps to your dream home, you notice the beautiful details: the stone work, the windows, the front door as it is opened for you.

As you walk deeper into your castle, you pass a room with a theater big enough for your family and friends, a kitchen designed by your personal chef, a music room with your grand piano, a dining room, a living room, your own library and even a pool room. Opulence engulfs you.

In moments, you find yourself standing in front of your walk-in closet, a wardrobe of wonder. It holds 100 outfits and 100 pairs of shoes. There are drawers filled with stylish clothes and accessories by designers from all over the world. Gucci. Armani. Versace. Ralph Lauren. Donna Karan. You have planned an elegant dinner party for this evening. All the details have been taken care of, and now all that remains is for you to get dressed for the evening.

Looking through the racks of designer wear, you choose a lightweight and elegant outfit. Putting on your clothes makes you feel like a million bucks, ready for the front cover of a magazine like GQ or *Vogue*. Three large mirrors show you that the clothes fit perfectly and that you look as good as you feel. Taking a moment to examine the images in the mirrors, you notice that you look calm, refreshed and healthy. You are relaxed and balanced and focused, ready to enjoy a special evening.

You walk through the halls toward the back of your mansion. You make your way outside and through the garden to the river that runs behind your property. This flowing waterway connects you to the waters of the world. Your luxury yacht is tied up to your dock. Its graceful lines and gleaming chrome mirror the details in your abundant life. You ascend the gangway, acknowledging the captain and the crew. They are ready for your signal. The guests are aboard; the evening can begin. Your guests admire you as you give the word to set sail toward the setting sun. Luxury and opulence engulf you.

The chef is supervising the preparation of dinner, and refreshments are being served. You are relaxed, calm and at peace. Everything you want to take place is happening as you had planned, as you wanted. Even as you are the host of this dinner, you feel like an honored guest, in the midst of the people who have helped you in the past; your family and friends, your coaches, teachers and mentors. All the important people of your past are with you, approving of the new direction. You have created an evening to remember.

VISUALIZING HAPPINESS: YOUR DREAM VACATION
Imagine your dream vacation. You've worked hard and earned some well-deserved time for rest and renewal. You can choose to go anywhere in the world, and the only limit you face is your imagination. Do you travel to the Caribbean, to delight in flying fish, rum and the sound of steel drums playing? Do you travel to Australia, to scuba dive along the vibrant waters of the Great Barrier Reef, exploring the outback in an open-air Jeep, then delighting in the sounds of the Sydney Opera House? Maybe you want to travel Europe by train, race camels between the Pyramids or travel up the Amazon by boat. Your life of abundance deserves to be abundant in pleasure, fun and relaxation. Maybe you decide to travel to Hawaii.

The moment has come. The phone rings; it is your gate man, announcing the arrival of the airport limousine. As you step outside, you feel the fresh morning air against your skin, as warm rays of sunlight welcome you to this day. It is early and the world is just awakening. You are filled with a sense of excitement about the days ahead.

You and your partner smile to each other as your bags are loaded quickly into the car; you've both been looking forward to this for some time. Your driver is polite and friendly. He offers you a complimentary newspaper, crisp and neatly folded. The car has been detailed and smells fresh. You enjoy a light morning snack as you are whisked away to the airport.

Upon arrival at the airport, your bags are quickly taken care of and you are invited to relax in the VIP lounge with the other first-class passengers. Relaxing music is playing in the background, and you are surrounded by other successful world travelers. People are chatting and effortlessly enjoying the moment. You enjoy the rare pleasure of unscheduled time. You can read, listen to your favorite music or write a note to a friend. You feel all the pressure melting away from you. A glass of sparkling champagne is offered to you along with your choice of bite-size delicacies to nibble on while you wait. You feel calm, centered and at peace. Life is the way it should be.

The plane you have chartered arrives and you board comfortably at your convenience. You sink back into the wide, leather chair and easily make yourself comfortable. In a few moments, the plane taxis out onto the runway. You feel your heart accelerate. The high-pitched sound of the engines fills the cabin. The plane thrusts forward suddenly and you feel yourself pressed back into your seat. Through the window, you watch the world streak by and tilt backward as the plane lifts off. The earth drops away from view. In moments, you burst upward through the sky and are surrounded by an ocean of soft, white, billowy clouds, bathed in bright sunlight. You and your partner settle in for the journey ahead.

After a few hours, you feel the plane slipping into its downward descent and the captain announces your impending arrival. Through the window, you see the blue ocean stretching as far as the eye can see, and it sparkles like diamonds glinting in the sun. Looming large in the distance is your destination, a tropical island paradise, its volcanic mountains stretching upward to touch the sky. The island is bathed in green vegetation, and the white foam of waves crashing along its coastline outlines its profile. The plane quickly makes its descent and taxis to a halt.

You have changed into lighter summer clothing, and the airplane door swings open. Warm tropical air bursts through the door to greet you. As you step out, the powerful yellow sun shines down on you, warming your skin and clothing. Palm trees line the distance, and you hear their leaves rustling as the wind gently washes through them. The breeze is comforting in the tropical warmth.

A tanned islander greets you with a bright smile and reaches over your head, setting a wreath of flowers around your neck. The petals are moist and soft to the touch, and you enjoy their fragrant scent. Your luggage has been loaded, and you are off to the hotel.

The lobby of your hotel is luxurious. Tropical plants explode upward from the ground. Cascading waterfalls cool the air, and the sound of the water is soothing. The décor is impeccable, perfect for this island paradise. You are offered a drink in the lobby and you savor the cool, tropical liquid. Your hotel check-in is smooth and effortless.

Your bags are carried promptly up to your room. Your room door is held open for you and you breezily stroll in. You are surrounded by opulence. Marble, gold and crystal highlight every surface. It feels as if the designer of the room had read your mind and knew exactly what you wanted the room to look like.

A kitchen area is provided if you prefer to do your own cooking, but you know that you can summon a gourmet chef to create a culinary masterpiece for you at your whim. You find a crystal bowl of chocolate-covered macadamia nuts welcoming you on the countertop. You enjoy some, tasting the chocolate as it melts on your tongue. A fresh tray of sliced pineapple is waiting beside it; the tangy bite of the sweet juice cleanses your palate. The hotel has made note of your special preferences in advance and has thoughtfully filled the fridge and shelves with all your favorite snacks. Looking around the room, you see that every amenity you can imagine has been provided.

Eagerly donning your swimsuit, you race downstairs and out onto the beach. The roar of the waves grows louder as you move quickly toward the tropical water. The white sand is hot beneath your bare feet. The crashing waves create a fine mist that tickles your skin. Standing at the edge of the water, the waves wash up and around your feet, causing you to sink into the sand. After a few moments, you wade out into the water; it is warm and inviting. You sink backward with a relaxed sigh into the warm waters of this tropical paradise, looking back at the opulent hotel, floating on your back in the blue ocean, with the yellow sun smiling down from above. You smile. Your vacation has now begun.

VISUALIZING LEGACY: GIVING BACK

You've decided it is time to give back. You've lived a life of abundance and you feel that to honor your great life worth you must share your prosperity with other souls. You decide to embark on an overseas mission that will serve those less fortunate and bring even greater significance to the material wealth you have accumulated. You have resolved to travel to a developing country, bringing medical supplies and helping with the construction of a school. Your spirit is overflowing with generosity. You know that you are blessed and that the greatest way to give thanks for your blessings is to invite others to bask in the sunlight of your success.

The first morning of your adventure finds you waiting at the airport with other like-minded souls. Some are rich in material wealth, some are abounding with physical vitality, some are gifted with heightened intellectual prowess and all are committed to a legacy act.

You see a vision of all the work you have done to create financial abundance, and in your mind you see the road you have traveled and how it has led you to this moment. Your wealth affords you the resources and flexibility to travel as you desire.

Your plane ride is uneventful, and after many hours and layovers you finally arrive at your destination. The spotless, stylish airport you departed from has been replaced with an aging airport filled with teeming crowds of people. Animals roam freely, sharing the roads with taxicabs and buses. The difference in wealth between your home country and this new land is startling, and you are glad you have come to bring some small measure of help. Your medical bags are cleared through customs and your missionary group boards an ancient school bus.

The next twelve hours find you leaving the main city and heading into the mountains. Corrugated metal rooftops adorn the tops of flimsy shacks, thrown together with mud and twigs. Even the dismal gray city seems rich in comparison. Your school bus thumps and lurches unsteadily, hitting every pothole for miles. As the sun burns a hole downward through the horizon, you notice there are no lights, no signs; you are absolutely cut off from all technology and civilization. You travel up a winding mountain pass through the night, and exhaustion forces you to drift off to sleep.

In the morning, you awake to discover a different world. You venture outside and stand on the road, with water streaming down what could be considered the curb. Animals move freely around the village, whether they are chickens, dogs or pigs. You smell the new aroma of spicy food wafting through open windows. Surrounding the village are the mountains that you traveled up, covered in dense green forest.

Villagers rush out of their homes to greet you, throwing their arms up to the sky and shouting thanks for the miracle of your arrival. Children laughing out loud dance around you, reaching out with their small hands to touch you. Grown men with tears in their eyes come out to shake your hand and through a translator give thanks for your presence. These people are rich in gratitude, thankful for every gift that life has offered them.

Over the coming weeks, you engage in a tireless effort with the others in your group to erect a new school by hand for these grateful townsfolk. It is the first time you've ever stirred concrete on the ground with a shovel, moved wheelbarrows filled with handmade bricks and spread concrete with a trowel. The concrete dust is sticky and refuses to be washed from your skin. The work places a great strain on your body yet offers a great release for your spirit. You learn to hammer thin metal rods into squares and use wire to tie them to 20-foot pieces of rebar. You are amazed that you are creating the support for a building that is rising from the ground because of your effort. You are amazed that you could derive so much spiritual pleasure from physical labor.

You feel the sun of this distant land setting the sky ablaze as the day moves forward. You celebrate your effort by enjoying a bottle of clean water. You relish splashing some water on your face, feeling it cool you in the midday heat.

When your meal breaks come, the physical exhaustion you experience has the magical ability to transform the food you eat into a gourmet experience. Every morsel of food is a delicacy. Every sip of water is a treasure. You laugh with the other missionaries at the delightful stories and priceless human moments of the day.

As the days spill into weeks, the shape and form of the school rises, brick by brick. At the end of your time here, you and the others stand proud in front of the new building you have created together through your own sweat and care. You embrace one another to capture the moment forever in your memories and honor each other's kindness in providing the town with the precious gift of a new school. Your success has been transformed into significance.

Action Steps

By visualizing your future, you are working to create the future you truly desire. It takes tremendous courage to admit what you really want out of life, because by doing so you risk disappointment and failure. If you never set a goal, you'll never experience the failure of not reaching it. But is it not the greater failure to fear failure and accept a life of mediocrity? You know you are destined for great things, and committing your goals to paper is the first step in making those goals materialize.

1. WHAT IS YOUR *ULTIMATE MISSION*? What small step could you take today to move toward it? How will you feel when you finally achieve this goal?

2. REVIEW YOUR *DESTINY CHECKLIST*. If there are any misalignments between the priorities that you profess to be important to you and the priorities that you actually spend time on, what can you do to change that? Select one priority that you feel you have neglected, and open up your calendar. Decide on a day in the next two weeks when you will take at least thirty minutes and spend it on the priority you feel you have neglected.

3. WHAT ARE YOUR *GOALS*? Make sure that you write them all out and always have the list in your sight. Print it and put it on every flat surface in your home. Are your goals logged in your virtual calendar? Are they posted on your desk for you to review daily? Which goal on the list is the goal that you will accomplish in the next ninety days? Which goal will you accomplish this year? What about in the next five years?

4. *VISUALIZE* YOURSELF HAVING ACHIEVED THE GOAL. Remember to use all your senses. Involve taste, touch, smell, sight and sound in your vivid visualization of your amazing future.

Now that you have a clear vision of what is possible, in the next chapter we will put a plan into action to lay the foundation for your new financial future. Prepare for a ruthless assessment of your current financial reality, but know that you will be given a toolbox to move you past challenges and into the black.

ACHIEVE FINANCIAL CERTAINTY

It is time to get absolutely real with where you are financially. We are going to take a clear, calculated and utterly honest look at the story that your financial statements are telling. We are going to go right back to the basics: tracking your spending habits; listing your expenses, assets, debts and net worth; and set up a budget. Every number that makes up your financial mosaic will be laid bare for ruthless examination. If you have dismissed this activity as rudimentary or put this exercise off in the past, today is the day for action. If you have justified inactivity with excuses, today is the day to focus on why you *must* follow through. "Procrastination" and "rationalization" are not words synonymous with wealth creation; "action" and "honesty" are. Getting straight about your money. Where you are. Where you are not.

We are going to work together over the coming pages to clear away the cobwebs and lay a new foundation for your financial future. You will come to a new way of relating to your financial situation — a financial consciousness driven by the facts as they are, not your interpretation of how they may be. I will share tools, strategies and behaviors that will remove chaos and bring structure to your financial habits. Combined with the concepts of the millionaire mindset, you will become unstoppable financially when you have laser-sharp clarity of your current situation.

You can't always delegate the management of your finances to advisors; at some point you have to step up and take ownership of your situation. We would never hire a fitness trainer to lift the weights for us; we hire them to encourage us so that we maximize our effort. Whoever does the work learns the lesson and grows the mental muscles. If your accountant is doing all the work, you'll never truly understand where you are or how you got there. It's time to roll up your own sleeves and get down to business.

Where Are You Now?

YOUR FINANCIAL GPS

A GPS (Global Positioning System) is a popular technology found in many smartphones and vehicles today. It is a brilliant service that receives information from a network of satellites orbiting the earth to tell you exactly where you are. If you're on a trip, a GPS allows you to enter the address of your desired destination and determine the best route to take, complete with a navigator dictating the directions, telling you when to turn left and when to turn right. Today, these systems are highly reliable and you can reasonably expect to be directed accurately to the front door of your destination.

Consider this: for the GPS to direct you successfully you must enter the address of where you want to go—your end goal. However, in order to reach your goal you must know exactly *where you are* so that your GPS device can plot an accurate path to your destination. Without knowing your current position, the GPS would be unable to direct you to your goal! Knowing where you are is not about looking around and getting a "sense" of where you believe you are, where you hope you are, where you think you are—it's about where you are precisely. Coordinates play such a critical role when spacecraft are re-entering the earth's atmosphere, when military planes are conducting an air raid or rescuing soldiers from the field of battle and when scuba divers are doing deep dives. Knowing where you are exactly can in many instances mean the difference between getting rescued or staying lost; between living or dying.

Reflect on the compelling analogy this draws to your current financial situation and the situation of which you dream. If you don't have your FPS (*Financial* Positioning System) working accurately, it is utterly impossible to plot a course toward your ultimate goals. You need to know how many dollars in liquid assets you have available for investment. You need to know how many dollars have already been saved. You need to know how many dollars are being needlessly consumed by high-interest debts. You need to know the percentage of dollars that are being lost to the oblivion of reckless purchases. In order for your flight to financial freedom to take off, you don't just require a destination city on your boarding pass—you need to know your departure gate!

FINANCIAL EXHAUSTION

"Financial Exhaustion" is the term I use when I meet people who aren't reaching their financial goals and are all too aware of this fact. These are people who may even know what they want in life; they've gone through a goal-setting exercise, they've gotten clear on their values, they know what actions they should take—and this knowledge is depressing because they realize they aren't following through on anything they've learned. To make matters worse, they're crushed by debt, overwhelmed by paperwork and depressed because of material lack. Their heart skips a beat when their credit card is run through the machine at any retail cash register, because they honestly don't know if it's going to clear. They lose sleep because they know that a big check is not going to clear the next day. Things have been this dreary for so long, they are just flat burned out from the pressure. Welcome to Financial Exhaustion.

You don't have to be that far gone to benefit from a thorough financial analysis and retooling. Regardless of your own particular situation, we're going to re-write your conversation with money. You know that you are meant to be wealthy. You know that our world is replete with opportunity, that we truly live in an abundant nation and that any amount of money is available for the person who masters the attitudes and behaviors of the rich. Do you choose *not* to lose sleep because of financial pressure and do you assert that you are ready to attract prosperity? Do you choose *not* to have money issues creating problems in your marriage when wealth should be fostering passion? Then get honest about answering these questions:

1. What are the financial stress points in your life? Where do you feel disconnected from aspects regarding money? What is not working as well as you'd like it to? Can you describe them?
2. What areas of your life are impacted by your responses above?
3. How would it feel to solve these financial disconnects forever?
4. Is there anything you would not be willing to do (as long as it's legal and moral) if you knew you could change your financial situation?

UNDERSTANDING YOUR FINANCIAL RESILIENCE

It is absolutely normal to face some financial obstacles along the path to success; however, when this happens most people choose to become demoralized and inactive. What sets champions apart is that they choose to surmount obstacles when they arise. If you want to create a truly magnificent life, you must be resilient in the face of adversity. Consider the following questions about how well you respond to financial setbacks.

1. What is the biggest financial challenge or "disaster" you have ever faced?

2. When this challenge struck, what thoughts went through your mind? Looking back on the situation, do you view that situation any differently today?

When You Face a Money-Related Challenge...

1. How would you describe your typical response, both mentally and behaviorally?

2. Would you say that you are able to remain calm in the face of adversity? Does it take you some time to calm down, or are you calm right away?

3. Do you ever really get upset? What financial situation would cause you to get upset? Why would you get upset over such a situation?

4. Do you ever imagine these situations as being bigger than they really are and blow them out of proportion?

5. Are you prone to worrying about finances? Do you think that worrying helps you take positive action or simply saps your energy and ruins your day?

6. Does life lose some of its enjoyment if you feel "beaten up" over a financial setback?

7. When you face a financial challenge, do you find it easy to forget your top priorities? Does this happen on a daily basis? Does abundance cause you to lose sight of your top priorities?

8. Does your pursuit of making money override your pursuit of your life's mission?

9. Do you believe that you will live a long life?

10. If you died tomorrow, do you feel that you've accomplished enough to honestly say you've lived a full life, or is there something that remains to be done?

11. On a scale of 1 to 10, rate your net worth versus your life worth. Which is higher?

12. Does it take unfortunate circumstances to make you stay focused on what matters most?

13. What major event has helped you to stay focused on your priorities?

14. What major event or obstacle has stood in the way of you having what you value most? How can you overcome this obstacle?

Fantasy, Faith or Fear: What Drives Your Pursuit of Wealth?

As much as some may profess to the contrary, people almost never accumulate wealth for the sake of having the *money*. People want to amass large fortunes because of what they believe the money will bring them. They are driven to become wealthy not for the cash, but for the proverbial payoff. So, what is driving you?

Some people might say, "I never want to worry again," and their driving force might be *security*. Some people might say, "I want to call the shots and never be controlled," and their driving force might be *freedom*. Others might say, "I want to make a difference in the world by building a youth center," and their driving force might be *philanthropy*. The force that compels us to accumulate wealth can also be driven by many of the factors we've discussed, such as self-esteem, attitudes toward money and belief in success. You must define what *you* believe money will give you, and how important that is for you. If you believe that money will give you security, what does security mean to you? If you believe that money will give you freedom, what does freedom mean to you?

When you finally experience wealth mastery, what will that mean for you in your life? Take a moment and consider the examples below. You may find that accumulating wealth is not a means of becoming happy, but that being happy is a means of becoming wealthy.

Take the "Money Will Give Me ..." Quiz

Simply put, what will having money bring to your life? Ponder this question in relation to each of the following, which are some of the most common wealth-drivers that people harbor. In each case, complete the sentence as it applies to you and your beliefs, checking the appropriate boxes:

"With enough money..."

Security

☐ My future is assured.

☐ Nothing can go wrong.

☐ We can handle any emergency.

Freedom/Choice/Control

☐ I can call all the shots in my life.

☐ No one can ever tell me what to do.

☐ I get to control my life.

Fun/Lifestyle/Leisure

☐ I can vacation wherever I want.

☐ I can wake up and go to bed as I please.

☐ I can buy whatever toys I fancy.

Power

☐ I get to tell people what to do.

☐ I can crush my competition.

☐ I can have pull with my local politicians.

Winning Recognition

☐ I'll get some respect from my family.

☐ People will be impressed with me.

☐ People will tell me how much they admire me.

To Provide for My Kids

- ☐ I'll be able to give my kids the advantages I didn't have.
- ☐ I'll get my kids into the best schools.
- ☐ I can make sure my kids are taken care of.

To Prove Something

- ☐ I'll show my teachers they were wrong about me.
- ☐ I'll prove to my parents that I can do it.
- ☐ I'll show everyone I was tough enough and smart enough.

Philanthropy

- ☐ I can help out those who are less fortunate.
- ☐ I will have a bigger purpose or quest in my life.
- ☐ I can make a difference in this world.

Self-worth

- ☐ I'll be a "somebody."
- ☐ I can make a difference in the world.
- ☐ I'll feel proud of myself.

Self-actualization

- ☐ I'll achieve all my dreams.
- ☐ I'll become the person I'm capable of being.
- ☐ There won't be any barriers to getting what I want.

Review your checkmarks and read the corresponding sections below to see what your selections say about you.

A. **SECURITY.** You believe that if you have enough money, nothing can ever go wrong. You know you'll be free from worry: you'll always have a roof over your head, food in your belly, clean clothing and the bills will be paid. If there is a downturn in the economy, you feel you will be immune. When the unexpected arises, you'll have the cash to manage it. You know that if anything happens to you, your loved ones will be taken care of financially. If you've watched your parents or peers go through economic hardship, you know your wealth will protect you from ever experiencing those challenges.

B. **FREEDOM/CHOICE/CONTROL.** You believe that with enough money you can control your life. No boss will ever push you around, because you will be the boss. No limits will be placed on your life that you can't surmount; you'll have the cash to do whatever you want. If you want to take off for ten days and go to Maui, not only will you have the cash in the bank to be able to do it, you won't have to ask anyone's permission. You will call the shots. Everything you've ever desired will be within reach.

C. **FUN/LIFESTYLE/LEISURE.** You believe that acquiring money will create a pleasurable lifestyle for you. You will drive a Pagani. You will partake of the finest dining. You'll be a VIP at the most exclusive clubs. You will be adorned with Versace and Armani. Whenever you travel, which will be often, you'll go first class. You'll become used to being waited on and treated like royalty. Life will be good!

D. **POWER.** You are driven to not only have control over your life but also over the lives of others. You believe that with sufficient wealth, you will have the full authority to captain your life and your business; you will be second fiddle to no one. You'll have the muscle to get things done. No one will be able to stake a claim in your territory without coming under your rule. Your supremacy will be assured with enough money.

E. **WINNING RECOGNITION.** You believe that if you make more money than most other people, then you'll have "won the game" and everyone is going to notice. You've been competing against your brother, your neighbor, your colleagues, your competitors, and now you will be "King of the Hill." When everyone else pulls up to their high-school reunion in their Honda Civic, you'll pull up in your Porsche 911. When you arrive at family get-togethers, everyone will be in awe of your exploits and lifestyle. When you purchase your new mansion, the local television crew will fly a helicopter over your estate and put the footage on the six o'clock news. You will be the talk of the town—because you'll be rich.

F. **TO PROVIDE FOR MY KIDS.** You feel that it's your duty and honor to give your kids what they need to have a strong start in life; after all, you love them. Maybe you want to give them advantages that you didn't have. Access to the elite schools. A fancy sports car when they turn 16. Prestige among their friends for living in the biggest house in town. A parent who shows them how to be successful by your own good example. The cash to help them start their own business, if they desire.

G. **TO PROVE SOMETHING.** You believe that if you make enough money, anyone who ever put you down is going to see their mistake. They are going to realize that you are tough enough, smart enough and savvy enough to pull off the big deals and really make it. You're going to show them. Your dad should have believed in you. Your mom should have been proud of you. Your schoolteacher should have encouraged you. Your ex should have stuck around. Your business competitors will be floored with the explosive growth of your enterprise. If anyone ever laughed at your ideas, they'll see. All the naysayers are going to see that you were right, and they were wrong. They'll eat their words.

H. **PHILANTHROPY.** You believe that the accumulation of wealth will allow you to help others. You feel the greatest good you can do with your wealth is to help those who can't help themselves. You know your life will have greater meaning and purpose through your contribution. You feel the gratitude in people's hearts when you uplift them and show them that they can turn away from a life of hopelessness to a life of possibility. Your wealth will allow you the time to volunteer wherever and whenever you want. If you want to take an afternoon and coach high-school kids on entrepreneurship through Junior Achievement, you'll be able to. If you want to help build a home locally through Habitat for Humanity, you'll be able to. If you want to get on a plane and build a school in a developing country, you'll be able to. If you want to build a summer camp for disadvantaged kids, you'll have the wealth to do it. If you want to pay for a new wing at your university or local hospital, you'll be able to. If you want to give a multi-million-dollar endowment to a charity, you'll be able to. Your wealth will allow you the opportunity to make a big difference.

I. **SELF-WORTH.** You believe that having money will make you a worthy or valuable person. Any self-esteem issues that you've faced in the past will be answered when you have a big enough bank account. You will finally be proud of yourself once you're rich. Even if people have praised you, now you'll know that you are equal to their compliments. Even if people already love you, you will finally feel deserving of their love.

> **J. SELF-ACTUALIZATION.** You believe that with money you can do, have and be everything you were meant to. You can truly come into your own. You feel that the giant lying inside you will be revealed to the world when you are rich. The greatness that is required to amass your wealth will pale in comparison to the greatness you will exude once you are rich. You will finally discover who you are; the real you will stand up and take a bow. You won't have to pretend to be something you're not; you'll have enough wealth to really be yourself. You'll be able to accomplish all the great things that you've imagined. You've always known you were meant to be rich, and you'll finally arrive at your proper destination. It is right to have choices. It is right to have your dreams. You were meant to reach your full potential.

Having completed this exercise, now consider these questions:

1. What is my #1 money-driver?
2. How much money will it take to finally get what I desire?
3. Is there any way that I could have more of what I want, today?
4. Is having this money-driver actually a barrier to my creating wealth?

The value in understanding what drives you is that you can use that information as leverage to motivate you to accomplish your goals. However, in my view, people tend to take money too seriously. In my mind, it's just a game. The only difference between talking about $100,000 and $100,000,000 is just a few zeros. But a hundred million dollars seems like such a big number for so many people. They create an automatic stop—a story inside their head called "That's Too Big." In order to acquire ample wealth, you must stretch your mind. To paraphrase Nobel Prize–winning author André Gide, to reach new lands, one must be willing to lose sight of the shore. To me, making money is the biggest, fastest game in the world, and your bank account is just there to keep score.

If I could give you any advice, it would be simply that you need to relax and allow money into your life. You need to change the conversation you are having in your own mind about money and rewrite your thoughts to say "Of course!" when a huge deal crosses your path. You need to expect it to work out. And when you are at peace with where you are, knowing that your current position is just a stepping stone on the pathway to greatness, all the blessings that you are chasing money for will flow so easily into your experience.

So, go after money if you feel it will give you security. Go after it if you feel it will give you power, or pride, or self-actualization or the ability to give back. Use these powerful motivators to drive you toward your goal. My greatest hope for you as you chase your dreams is that you realize that so many of the things you desire in life are already available to you today; money will simply make the trip more fun.

Now we're going to get really introspective and identify your current behaviors and the beliefs that drive them. You are going to see with utter clarity exactly where you are on track, and where you have gone awry. Some people really enjoy understanding why they are in their current position financially, and some people like to use the "ostrich maneuver" and bury their heads in the sand, avoiding the problem. The following quiz is going to remove any sand from your eyes so that you can see the truth — and then we're going to rewrite your truth to create the future you desire. Let's get started!

The "Money Management" Quiz

Using a gearshift analogy, take out a pen and check off every sentence that describes your behaviors and beliefs toward money.

In Reverse

- ☐ Creating a budget is a waste of time; I never follow it anyway.
- ☐ It's too complicated to keep my bills organized.
- ☐ I feel overwhelmed when I think about my debt situation.

- [ ] I carry a balance on my credit card(s).
- [ ] I only make minimum payments.
- [ ] I am sometimes late in making bill payments.
- [ ] I sometimes bounce checks and incur NSF charges.
- [ ] I must borrow money or use credit cards to pay my bills.
- [ ] I owe money to my friends and family.
- [ ] I can't seem to make it to payday without borrowing cash.
- [ ] I've needed to consolidate debt payments.
- [ ] I use a cash advance against my paycheck each week.
- [ ] I worry that I won't have the money to pay my bills.
- [ ] When I shop, sometimes I'm not sure if I have enough money available to make the purchase.
- [ ] I avoid reading my mail because I dislike receiving late payment notices.
- [ ] When I'm having a bad day, shopping makes me feel happy.
- [ ] I've been working hard, so I deserve to buy a new toy.
- [ ] The overdraft in my bank account is actually "my money."

In Park

- [ ] I'm not borrowing any money...
- [ ] I'm also not saving any money!
- [ ] The bills are being paid... barely.
- [ ] I never have any cash left over for long-term investments.
- [ ] I feel good when I make a bill payment.
- [ ] I feel good that I'm making all the minimum payments on my debts.
- [ ] I'm living paycheck to paycheck.
- [ ] If I keep doing what I'm doing, five years from now *nothing* will have changed.
- [ ] I know that something *has* to change.
- [ ] I feel concerned about my lack of savings for the future.
- [ ] I'm scared of the compound interest on my credit cards and try to avoid using them.
- [ ] I don't dip into the overdraft on my bank account.

In First Gear

- ☐ I keep my receipts and write down every purchase.
- ☐ I've called a credit bureau to request a copy of my credit report.
- ☐ When I get my bills, I enter the information into my financial management software.
- ☐ I balance my checkbook every time I get my statement.
- ☐ I take pride in saying "no" to impulse purchases.
- ☐ When I go grocery shopping, I only buy the items that are on my written list.
- ☐ I have a monthly budget prepared, and I regularly follow it.
- ☐ I have a written list of all of my debt payments.
- ☐ I am attacking my debt and paying it down.
- ☐ I like to read books on managing money.
- ☐ I consider myself a wise shopper.
- ☐ If there is a way of spending less, I'm interested.
- ☐ I have extra cash in my bank account at the end of the week.
- ☐ I don't believe in buying on credit; I like to pay cash.
- ☐ If I don't have the money, I don't deserve to buy non-necessities.
- ☐ Toys, fun and entertainment are part of my budget.
- ☐ I know exactly how much I owe, my total net worth and my amount of available cash.

In Second to Fourth Gears

- ☐ I have a financial planner with whom I meet regularly.
- ☐ I have clearly defined long-term savings plans.
- ☐ My friends and family admire my ability to manage money.
- ☐ I have several months of income saved in case of emergency.
- ☐ I have my will prepared.
- ☐ I am well insured for my home, health, life and car.
- ☐ A certain percentage of my income is automatically deducted from my paycheck and deposited into my RRSP.
- ☐ I feel just as much pleasure saving money as I do spending it, if not more.

- ☐ I follow the stock market and want to be an educated investor.
- ☐ I attend courses on creating wealth through vehicles such as real estate and investing in stocks.
- ☐ I am successfully saving to be able put my kids through university.
- ☐ My mortgage is being paid off aggressively.
- ☐ I pay off my credit cards in full every month and never carry a balance.
- ☐ I feel confident keeping cash in my billfold, knowing that it will not be spent impulsively.
- ☐ I associate with people who are good at managing their money.

In Fifth Gear

- ☐ In addition to planning for security and comfort, I am following a plan for creating wealth.
- ☐ I have a high emotional tolerance to risk.
- ☐ I make it a point to associate with wealthy people.
- ☐ I regularly meet with my friends and colleagues to discuss wealth-creation strategies.
- ☐ Wealth-creating opportunities regularly present themselves.
- ☐ I have an "abundance" mentality.
- ☐ I take calculated risks with money...
- ☐ ...but never threaten my plan for basic retirement savings and comfort.
- ☐ I have identified and eliminated any negative beliefs about money that may have held me back in the past.
- ☐ I have enough money to retire any time I want, so I am able to do what I love with my time.
- ☐ I am considered a sophisticated investor.
- ☐ I live on a small percentage of my income and invest the rest.
- ☐ I have a small team of trusted tax attorneys and accountants.
- ☐ I leverage my home's equity to build more wealth.
- ☐ I am successfully self-employed or own a business.

Congratulations on completing the quiz! Whichever section contains the most checked-off boxes will indicate where your own beliefs and behaviors regarding money currently fall—which gear you're in. Your aim is to *transition* from one level to the next, until you are finally in fifth gear and speeding toward your vision of the ultimate future! However, it's important to note that you can't go from reverse to first: you'll blow the engine or transmission. You can drive in low gears, at high RPMs, and risk damaging the engine for the long run—or you can make the brave transition, commit to the actions necessary and engage the next gear.

Similarly, you can't just go from first gear to fifth: you'll stall out on the highway. The natural progression of your path to personal financial mastery is going to involve learning new tools and habits at each stage, and these habits will build on top of one another. You will probably find that your journey has you moving fairly consistently from one gear to the next in the order they were designed, building on the momentum of the last gear you were in. Now, let's review each category in detail.

Reverse

It's time for a reality check: things are bad and getting worse. If you don't take immediate action, you are going to suffer tremendous financial setbacks. You avoid opening the mail because it's probably a bill you can't pay. You don't want to answer the phone because the credit collectors are calling day and night. You're worried that all the things you bought with credit will be repossessed. Almost assuredly your present financial reality is based upon your thinking and actions—and you can turn these around as soon as you choose. You have to make the decision that *things must change!*

Park

You've numbed or neutralized yourself out of action, experiencing financial resignation. You know well enough that when you're in a financial hole, you need to stop digging. You've only got lint in your wallet, but at least you can retain some pride for not charging things on credit. The thought of getting out of this mess seems a little far off and impossible at the moment. You're basically in survival mode, living paycheck to paycheck—and at the present rate of improvement, you expect to be in this situation for a long time.

First Gear

You're forming some good habits and you have financial awareness. You're getting more organized and disciplined about tracking your expenses, purchasing according to your plan and living within your means. You're starting to pay off your credit cards. You don't buy things on impulse anymore. The numbers in your checkbook are finally adding up! However, you are aware that you don't have the savings for your future that you would like. You're putting a few dollars away, but not enough to achieve your long-term goals.

Second to Fourth Gears

You are now thinking long term. Second gear: you have financial direction and a definitive course of action. Third gear: you have financial momentum and a portfolio on purpose. Fourth gear: you have a new capital consciousness. You are adopting the beliefs and strategies of sound money management. You have a firm appreciation of the power of compound interest and will never allow procrastination to halt your progress again. You meet regularly with your financial advisor and have a clear plan for your financial future. You know exactly how much money is required for you to maintain your lifestyle at retirement and are investing in that plan on a regular basis. If you have children, the money for their education is also being saved according to plan. All the i's are dotted and the t's are crossed: your will is prepared, you are fully insured and your paperwork is in order. However, you yearn for more than just security. Your plan will provide you with a secure future, but not an extravagant one. There are still places to see and things to do, and you are aware that your plan allows you a modest lifestyle, but not the future of your dreams. You require a plan for creating real wealth.

Fifth Gear
You are on cruise control for capital creation. You have graduated past mere security being your chief financial goal in life; now your sights are set on creating real wealth. You are thinking big and seeing all the possibilities a life without limits can offer. You have a mastermind team of financial advisors, tax attorneys and lawyers whom you meet with regularly to assure your financial victory. You associate with wealthy people and the topic of conversation is the next business opportunity that will line your pockets with profit. Your risk tolerance is increasing daily. Making money is the biggest game in town and you love playing the game to win. Money doesn't scare you; it's just a way of keeping score. You are focused on building businesses, real estate investments and other opportunities not available to the unsophisticated investor.

Have you made the decision to step up and get into full gear? I'm going to take you step by step through the principles and practices of moving up to fifth gear. By the time we're done, you'll understand exactly what to do to manage your money, define your future and create the wealth you desire. Let's begin at the beginning: moving you from reverse into first gear by tracking your spending.

If You Can Track It, You Can Change It
The first step in personal financial mastery is laying all your cards on the table and surveying what hand you are holding. Some of your financial cards have been dealt by chance; some have been dropped by choice. Regardless of the path you've taken to arrive

in your current situation, you are where you are. The only value in reviewing the past and saying "I should have" or "If only I'd" is to reap lessons for the purpose of applying them in the future. It's not about the act of recording the facts, or curbing your spending. It's like *The Karate Kid*—wax on, wax off; breathe in, breathe out—building foundational consciousness. In other words, becoming aware. This is what fuels responsibility.

I'm going to help you navigate some elementary financial steps to assess your financial "state of the nation." Below you'll find a financial template to record your expenses. Your monthly expenses will consist of fixed, variable and miscellaneous expenses.

Fixed Monthly Expenses

This will include the large and small bills for which you know exactly what you will be charged each month. These bills likely consume a large portion, if not the bulk, of the money that you direct toward personal expenses. Examples of these bills are your mortgage payment (or rent), car payment, insurance (car, home and life) payments and other large recurring bills.

Variable Monthly Expenses

These figures will include bills that you can reasonably expect to pay each month, but the amount is variable instead of fixed. One month you may pay $100, the next month $300, and the next month you may pay $225. Examples of these expenses would include groceries, utilities, gasoline, cell phone and so on. They would also include bills that you pay every second or third month, such as property taxes and professional fees. For each of these expenses, add up several months and determine an estimated average. This is the number that you will put into your budget. The greater period of time that you average these numbers over (for example, six to twelve months), the greater the likelihood of accuracy in your average.

Miscellaneous Expenses

This final category will contain all the bills that may be more random, and certainly less of a prerequisite for your survival (although you might debate this point!). This category could contain items such as entertainment, clothing, vacations and a myriad of small purchases (lunch, soda pop, a coffee, a magazine, a newspaper, etc.). There may not seem to be a pattern to your purchasing, and the items might seem too small to even bother noticing on a budget — but everything adds up.

Financial Tracking Sheet

Monthly Expenses

Home		Personal	
Mortgage/Rent	$ _____	Groceries	$ _____
Property Taxes	$ _____	Gym Membership	$ _____
Home Maintenance	$ _____	Health & Beauty	$ _____
Home Decoration	$ _____	Pet Expenses	$ _____
Gas Heating	$ _____	Clothing	$ _____
Electricity	$ _____	Retirement Savings	$ _____
Water	$ _____	Education/Tuition	$ _____
Telephone	$ _____	Emergency Fund	$ _____
Cell Phone	$ _____	Child Care	$ _____
Cable	$ _____	Laundry/Dry Cleaning	$ _____
Internet	$ _____	Life Insurance	$ _____
Home Insurance	$ _____	Medical Expenses	$ _____
		Medicine/Prescriptions	$ _____
Automobile		Dental/Vision	$ _____
Vehicle Payment	$ _____	Clothing	$ _____
Gasoline	$ _____	Entertainment	$ _____
Car Maintenance	$ _____	Restaurants	$ _____
Car Insurance	$ _____	Tobacco	$ _____
		Alcohol	$ _____
		Gifts	$ _____
		Travel	$ _____
		License/Dues	$ _____
		Kids' Education Fund	$ _____
		Charity Donations	$ _____
		Hobbies	$ _____
		Kids' Activities/Sports	$ _____

Now, here is where the game really begins. It is very simple to record how much your home costs you; it is much more laborious to track how much cash you drop on the $5 and $10 dollar purchases, let alone the $1 ones. "Why bother tracking these little expenses?" you scoff; "Don't you know how much money I make?" Yes, certainly you are successful and doing well. The point is, though, it doesn't matter how much you *earn*; what matters is how much you *keep*.

If you make $1 million but you spend $2 million, then you're broke! And the guy who indiscriminately treats his friends to beer and wings when he's making $50,000 won't think twice about treating them to ski lessons and spa retreats when he's making $500,000. Your habits will carry forward regardless of your income, and knowing where your money is going is simply an entry-level skill when it comes to money management.

Let's say you are an employee and you get paid every second Friday. Many people in this kind of situation don't have the self-control to manage the tiny purchases. They go through a standard ritual: the paycheck goes into their bank account, they are flush with cash ... and all of a sudden they start facing some dire financial emergencies. Serious emergencies! Like, the "leather jacket emergency," or the "take your spouse out to live theater emergency" or the "plasma screen home theater emergency." It's amazing how we are stricken with such dire crises as these when our wallet starts to get a little fat! Every toy we've lusted after is now within striking distance. You've got some cash in your hands and now you're picking up that new suit that you saw in the store window, that new tablet with just the right features, and a new outfit for your Paris-Hilton-esque toy dog. Then, when Monday inevitably rolls around, you cry, "Where did all my money go?!"

The reason to track every single purchase is so that we have an answer to this question. So what I'm going to encourage you to do is to start carrying a pen and a notepad with you and quite literally write down absolutely everything you buy. If you prefer, type it into your BlackBerry or smartphone. It doesn't matter how you track your numbers, it just matters that you do it. It is a good idea to use your debit card for purchases so that you have an electronic copy of your purchase, and the data can later be imported into money management software to track your expenses more accurately. You may also use a credit card (for example, if you are saving up for points on a reward program card), but if you do so you must ensure that you are going to immediately put the money you use back onto the credit card. If you use cash, you must handwrite (or type) every purchase in the log you're carrying.

Here is what is going to happen: in the beginning, if you actually do this exercise, you may feel hesitant about making some purchases that you normally wouldn't balk at. Why? Because you are pausing for a moment to ask, "Do I really need this? Do I really want a record of having wasted money on this thing? Is this the smartest financial decision, long term?" As soon as you start asking yourself questions like these, your purchasing habits will change overnight. A powerful way to increase your likelihood of follow through is to give a copy of your monthly expense report to a trusted friend who will hold you accountable. Knowing that someone else will know that you've wasted money on something silly might just be the thing you need to deter you from making the purchase.

However, try in the beginning to actually make the same purchases that you normally do. Why? Because if you are on your best behavior for two weeks and only make wise purchases, then at the end of the exercise you will be no closer to unraveling the mystery of where your money escapes to. You need some cold hard data in order to really understand the flow of your in-pocket cash.

If and when you complete this exercise, and you've been honest and thorough, you are going to discover something: that you are *stunned* where you are spending money and how much of it is flowing out of your pocket into the pockets of merchants — money you could be investing or using to launch new opportunities. You won't believe how much cash you are blowing on silly purchases!

The real number you are ultimately concerned about is your *net worth*. You never read the *Forbes* list of billionaires to hear about their salary; you want to know their net worth. $10 million? $50 million? $100 million? Salary is secondary to the wealthy. The wealthy always know their numbers, and they are always focused on the total amount that they own.

Understand that every purchase you make is either increasing or decreasing your net worth. When you buy a donut, your net worth goes down by a dollar or two. Some purchases are investments that temporarily decrease your net worth, but over the long haul they will increase your net worth. What you don't want to be doing is frivolously frittering away your money on needless things. Every time you save instead of spend, you secure that money to survive another day and grow.

One fascinating question to consider is this: *How much money have you earned over your lifetime?* If you've been working twenty years making $100,000 a year, you've earned $2 million. After having earned that much cash, what do you have to show for it? Because the key to net worth is not how much you make, it's how much you keep! Over the next twenty years, how much do you intend to earn, and how much do you intend to keep? I'm going to share some strategies on how to keep more and more of your wealth—starting right now.

How to Manage Your Money

I'm shocked at how some successful six-figure professionals live paycheck to paycheck with no real savings or long-term investment. Mind you, they've got the hot new luxury car parked in the driveway ... leased. They've got the motorboat tied up at their cottage dock ... purchased on credit. They eat at the finest restaurants, wear the latest fashions, and their lifestyle is burning them into the ground. With so much information available today on basic financial principles, I'm going to take just a moment and review some fundamental principles as a refresher for you; daily habits and strategies that help in the creation and maintenance of wealth. If you aren't practicing these principles today, ask yourself why, and what the long-term cost might be. Sound financial management applies to $100,000 just as it applies to $10,000,000. The top principles I'm going to discuss are:

1. Pay Yourself First
2. Avoid the Credit Card Habit
3. Know Your Credit Rating
4. Make One Big Payment
5. Eliminate Your Mortgage
6. Utilize the Power of Compound Interest
7. Sleep on Your Purchases

1. *Pay Yourself First*

People tend to be motivated by avoiding pain. If there is an immediate unwanted consequence to an action, the majority of individuals will go out of their way to avoid this discomfort. However, when the consequence is far in the future and poses no immediate threat, the average person will refuse to accept responsibility and delude themselves by saying, "I'll get to it later." For this reason, you must pay yourself first. Before you pay the mortgage, the water bill, your taxes — before all else — put money into your long-term investment plan.

The reason to do this is because you face no immediate consequence if you fail to make the deposit. If you don't invest in your RRSP today, who's going to complain? Really, no one. However, if you bounce your mortgage payment, you're going to be getting a message from the bank that afternoon. You are highly motivated to avoid the pain of missed responsibilities when other people are holding you accountable. In order to stay on track, make your first payment to your own future.

The simplest way of doing this is to have money deducted on a weekly or bi-weekly basis from your account, ideally when you expect a paycheck. The money should be automatically transferred into one of your investment vehicles. Select an amount of money that is challenging but realistic; don't save $1 when you can save $1,000. By having the money electronically transferred automatically, it is out of sight and out of reach.

A good target percentage of your income is 10 percent. In George Samuel Clason's *The Richest Man in Babylon*, we learn that when we live on 90 percent of our income we really don't notice the difference in lifestyle; we adjust very quickly. If you can invest 10 percent of your income every two weeks, you are well on your way to securing financial independence. More importantly, you are practicing the important art of self-denial by choosing willingly to live beneath your means — a habit that will serve you well when your means have expanded 100-fold.

2. Avoid the Credit Card Habit

In order to live abundantly, you must do so on your terms, not the terms of your creditors. Many people choose to buy things using their credit card. Their short-term indulgence is rewarded with long-term bondage to their interest payments. And when a person receives their credit card statement in January reminding them of their December shopping spree, do you think they look to pay off the full amount? Most people don't; their eyes gaze longingly at the two magic words that enable their financial descent: "Minimum Payment." If you make only a minimum payment, do you know how long it will take you to pay off your credit cards? Consider this: "A $1,000 charge on an average credit card will take almost 22 years to pay off and will cost more than $2,300 in interest ($3,300 total), if only 2 percent minimum payments are made."[1]

Many people carry debt levels of $5,000, $10,000, even $20,000 on their credit cards, and it will literally take decades to pay off the amount. Suze Orman, financial guru and frequent guest columnist in *O, The Oprah Magazine*, says, "When you go to purchase something on credit, just imagine it costs *five times as much!*" So if you see a new shirt for $100, you need to ask yourself if it would be worth owning if the price were five times as much. When you realize how compound interest is working against you, you're likely to make different buying decisions.

3. *Know Your Credit Rating*

If you don't know where you stand, you may not have a sense of urgency about paying down your high-interest debts. The worst time to discover that you have a weak credit rating is when you are sitting across from your banker looking for a loan: they pull up your credit report and have to say "sorry" to your request. You want to find out exactly where you stand, and also double-check that there are no inaccuracies. You want to understand exactly how your credit is being rated by various reporting agencies. It is entirely possible that you've paid off a debt but your final payment has not been reported to the credit bureau and the outstanding debt is still appearing on your credit report. You can get a copy of your report by contacting any credit reporting service. One such service is Equifax.

4. *Make One Big Payment*

When you make the decision to attack your personal debt, I recommend this strategy: instead of thinking of your various debts as separate, consider combining them in your mind into one big payment.

1 Paul Bannister, www.bankrate.com

In order to do this, you want to first list all of your current debts, their interest rates and the monthly payments. *List them in order of each debt's interest rate, from highest to lowest.* Then list the total amount owing and your average monthly payment for all outstanding debts. Now, add up all the monthly payments to arrive at a single figure: the total monthly payment on debt. What you are now going to do is simple: instead of thinking of your debts as five to ten separate payments, you are going to think of them as *one big payment.* Consider the following chart:

Sample Debt Chart				
Creditor	Annual Interest Rate*	Total Due	Daily Interest Rate*	Monthly Payment
MasterCard	24%	$5,000.00	0.06557%	$101.64
Visa	18%	$5,000.00	0.04918%	$76.23
Amex	15%	$5,000.00	0.04098%	$63.52
Discover	12%	$5,000.00	0.03279%	$50.82
Credit line	8%	$5,000.00	0.02186%	$33.88
Total		$25,000.00	$3,850.00	$326.09

* Rates are examples only, for the purpose of illustration.

A few comments about credit card interest:

- Credit cards calculate the daily interest rate.
- "Daily interest" is calculated by dividing the annual rate by the number of days in the year (i.e., 365).
- Any given purchase not paid off 100 percent by the due date will be attributed with interest based on the days between the date it was purchased to the date of the next bill, times the daily interest rate.

- Unpaid balances plus unpaid interest are continuously attributed with additional interest each succeeding month.
- Many credit cards charge an annual fee of $100 to $150.
- Thus, the monthly fee listed in the simple example I provided is likely going to increase and you'll need to adjust your plan accordingly.

So, now that you've listed your numbers, here's what you do: every single month you pay that one big total amount, and you *never deviate from paying that amount* until every debt is paid off. Then, each month, after making the one big payment, you take every extra dollar you have and attack the first item in your list of debts until it is eliminated. Where does the extra money come from? Well, for starters, it can come from your miscellaneous expenses, all of the bills that you have a lot of choice and flexibility about. You can't change your mortgage payment tomorrow, but you can choose whether or not to dine in your favorite restaurant or go shopping for a new outfit. Also, it could come from extra money that you earn. There is no need to reduce your lifestyle if you can generate the money you need! Go ahead and work harder, sell more, close another deal—whatever you need to do.

If you owe money on something that isn't a necessity, *consider returning the product.* If you've purchased a couch, new entertainment system, Jet Ski, hot tub, or anything else that you are making payments on, the wisest thing might be to swallow your pride and take one step back in order to take two steps forward. You shouldn't get in the habit of financing your lifestyle; all of these things are great to have but you need to pay cash for them. If you have a slowdown in business for a few months, the debt payments on these luxury items are going to eat you alive. Have a sale and clear this stuff out if necessary.

You may also *consider moving some of your high-interest credit card debt to a credit line with a lower interest rate.* In a way, by doing this you are consolidating your own loans. But beware! You can't then just give yourself free rein to go on a shopping spree with your whistle-clean credit card. You are going to spiral downward into bankruptcy if you manage your money that way. What you need to do after you've consolidated is cut up the credit card or stuff it in the back of your closet. Get it out of sight where it can't do any damage. You've got to take control of your spending and not dig your hole any deeper.

As you attack the first payment on your list with focus, you will be stunned by how fast you can pay it off. Now, look what has happened: since you've paid off the first item on the list, you no longer have to make a payment each month of, using the chart above as an example, $101.64. So what do you do with this newly discovered money? Well, most people take the money and run. They head right to the shopping mall and come home with a new pair of shoes. What you need to understand is that you must continue to make *one big payment* each month, and never deviate. The payment didn't go down by $101.64 this month; the payment stays the same. Instead, you take the extra $101.64 and apply it directly to the principal of the next item on the list. By doing this, you dramatically accelerate the debt-reduction process and you'll be out of your credit card debt in no time.

5. *Eliminate Your Mortgage*

Once you have eliminated your personal high-interest debt, the next major debt for most people is their mortgage. We leave this debt for last because mortgage rates are generally much lower than personal credit cards, and the amount owing is usually the largest debt a person has. The term mortgage literally means "agreement until death," which is how long many people take to pay off their house! It is common for people to have 25-year mortgages, but some banks are even offering 30- and 35-year mortgages. This is astounding. Whatever your current age, imagine adding 35 years to that number, and that would be when you would pay off such a loan. I can't even imagine being in bondage to a credit company for that period of time. And what is the reward that tempts people to take such a destructive action? The thought of saving about $100 a month on their payments.

Now, I'll let you in on a secret: imagine what would happen to your lifestyle if you didn't have a mortgage payment each month and all of a sudden that cash could be spent on other things. Would that make a difference in your life? Absolutely! Clearly then, it's in your best interest to reduce the length of your mortgage by as many years as possible, by paying it off more quickly. Let's say, for example, you pay $2,000 a month on your mortgage. If you look at this example strictly mathematically, if you double your monthly payment and begin paying $4,000 a month on a 30-year mortgage, you won't cut the time it takes to pay off your debt down to fifteen years—*you will cut it down to roughly six years*. Let me repeat that: if you double your mortgage payment, then mathematically speaking, a 30-year mortgage will be reduced to roughly six years. Now, the banks won't allow this, for reasons I'll go on to explain, but the chart below helps to illustrate the concept.

The Effect of a Shorter Amortization Period

Mortgage Amount	$100,000	$100,000	$100,000	$100,000
Amortization period	25 years	20 years	15 years	10 years
Monthly principal and interest payment	$639.81	$712.19	$839.89	$1,106.51
Interest cost over amortization period	$91,842.27	$70,851.88	$51,123.89	$32,740.99
Interest savings over amortization period	$0.00	$20,990.59	$40,718.58	$59,101.48

This chart is for illustrative purposes only and assumes an interest rate of 6% over the amortization period.

Isn't the difference amazing? However, lending companies and banks have an insurance policy against you in case you read a book like this and learn this interesting little fact, and that insurance policy is called a "pre-payment penalty." I'm sure you are familiar with this term. It means that if you try to pay off your house faster than agreed, you will be financially penalized. So here is what you do to work around this obstacle.

First, call your bank or mortgage broker and request a copy of your *current amortization chart*. (You may also be able to access it online.) This is the chart that shows the number of dollars each month from your mortgage payment that goes toward paying down the principal and the portion that goes to pay down the interest. Most people are sickened when they realize that after a year of paying they've basically only paid off the door knob—and after a decade they've paid off their front door. But you need to know these numbers in order to attack your debt effectively.

Next, review the details of your mortgage. What is the maximum amount you are allowed to pay each month on your mortgage without incurring a pre-payment penalty? Whatever the figure is, now that you've paid off your credit cards you've got the extra cash to tackle this last debt. Determine the maximum you are allowed to pay, and *start paying the maximum monthly amount*. If your mortgage has a once-a-year option of paying a lump sum, or an option to increase the amount, do it. Then arrange to meet with your bank; you want to renegotiate these numbers and increase the amount you are able to pay each month without penalty. Remember, you are their customer and the product they are offering can be purchased across the street at another bank. If you don't like the terms of your mortgage, renegotiate or consider finding a new lender, keeping in mind that breaking your mortgage would incur a fee, likely a few months of interest, so these numbers need to be factored into your decision.

Next, if you are paying on a monthly basis, switch to *making a payment every two weeks* or paying once a week. Most paychecks cycle every second Friday, so it will fit more easily into your budget to have the money deducted automatically on payday. And you won't notice the difference in your lifestyle if you have to pay every 28 days versus 30 or 31; it will be very easy to adjust to and you will save additional money.

The Effect of Increasing the Frequency of Your Payments

Number of Payments per Year	Payment Amount	Interest over the Term	Principal Balance at End of Term	Amortization Remaining after the 5-Year Term	Years of Payments Saved over the Life of Mortgage
Monthly—12	$639.81	$28,232.54	$89,843.94	20 years	0 years
Biweekly—26	$319.91	$27,625.36	$85,953.49	15 years, 11 months	4 years, 1 month
Weekly—52	$159.96	$27,597.72	$85,924.58	15 years, 10.5 months	4 years, 1.5 months

This chart is for illustrative purposes only. Assumes a $100,000 mortgage with an amortization period of 25 years and an initial interest rate of 6% over a five-year term.

Another way of accelerating your debt reduction is to *add next month's principal to your mortgage payment this month*. Let's say your amortization chart says that next month, your mortgage payment of $2,000 has $100 dollars that will be applied to the principal. Here's what to do: this month, pay $2,000 plus the $100 principal for next month. What does this accomplish? It eliminates all of the interest on next month's payment, or $1,900. You will *never* pay the $1,900.

In saying this, a reverse concept should be discussed: *Never miss a payment.* If your bank says, "Hey, it's Christmastime and we know that money is tight because you're out shopping—so if you want to skip a payment, no problem!" Do not *ever* do this. You will add months and months of additional payments to your mortgage, even as much as or more than a year of additional payments. It's not worth it.

If you are a first-time homebuyer, you can also do this: on the day you get your mortgage, on that very day when you sign the papers and the mortgage company gives you your money, *that very day—immediately give the lender your first month's payment.* By the way, they will fight you on this. They will say, "No, you need to make this payment 30 days from now." Insist that they take your money. The lender will say, "Let's just roll the money you are giving us into your down payment." Do not listen to them; pay your first month's payment the second you get your mortgage. Why? Because the interest on your home is compounded daily. When you make a mortgage payment the moment you get the money, the clock hasn't started ticking on the interest. This means that 100 percent of the money you pay will be directed toward the principal. This will be the one and only time that 100 percent can attack the principal, so don't waste the opportunity!

6. *Utilize the Power of Compound Interest*
Albert Einstein is known for having many memorable quotes, but there's one in particular that will help emphasize my next point: "Compound interest is the eighth wonder of the world." Compound interest is a powerful ally in the pursuit of wealth—but it can also be a crippling adversary if it's working against you. For, once you are in the throes of high-interest debt, it is a laborious and consuming ordeal to wrench yourself free of its shackles.

In order to fully appreciate the power of compound interest, you need to run some numbers and see how the money adds up over a long period of time. While it's true that much of the world in 1626 had no exposure to financial instruments like compound interest, the power of compound interest is illustrated in this example:

If the Native American tribe that accepted goods worth 60 guil-
ders [roughly $16] for the sale of Manhattan in 1626 had in-
vested the money in a Dutch bank at 6.5% interest, compounded
annually, then in 2005 their investment would be worth over
€700 billion (around US $1,000 billion), more than the assessed
value of the real estate in all five boroughs of New York City.
With a 6.0% interest, however, the value of their investment to-
day would have been €100 billion (7 times less!).[2]

And that is just a 0.5 percent difference in the examples!

To quickly determine what your return would be, a simple mathematical formula you can use is the Rule of 72. This helps determine the approximate number of years it will take for your money to
double. Simply put, let's say you invest $1,000 at 9 percent. You div-
ide the number 72 by the interest rate to determine the number of
years till it doubles. Seventy-two divided by nine is eight, thus it will
take approximately 8 years for your money to double. So in 8 years
you will have $2,000, in 16 years you will have $4,000, in 24 years you
will have $8,000, and so on.

To further explore the power of compound interest, you can
make use of various calculators online.[3] Consider taking $100 every
two weeks and investing it at 6 percent, 9 percent and 12 percent
respectively over 30 years. The results are astounding. If you have
not yet done so, I would recommend that you sit down with
your financial advisor and run some numbers based upon your
own goals and budget. I'm sure that the numbers you hear will be
compelling! Following are some different examples for illustrative
purposes only:

2 "Compound Interest; history," www.wikipedia.com
3 http://www.bygpub.com/finance/InterestCalc.htm

$50 Invested Weekly at 6% Compound Interest

Year	Value
1-year value (total value of your account at the end of one year)	$ 2,678.03
2-year value (total value of your account at the end of two years)	$ 5,521.67
3-year value (and so on ...)	$ 8,541.15
4-year value	$ 11,747.34
5-year value	$ 15,151.80
10-year value	$ 35,604.59
15-year value	$ 63,212.98
20-year value	$ 100,480.40
30-year value	$ 218,691.83
40-year value	$ 434,087.11
50-year value	$ 826,562.88

$100 Invested Weekly at 6% Compound Interest

Year	Value
1-year value (total value of your account at the end of one year)	$5,356.07
2-year value (total value of your account at the end of two years)	$11,043.35
3-year value (and so on ...)	$17,082.31
4-year value	$23,494.69
5-year value	$30,303.60
10-year value	$71,209.19
15-year value	$126,425.97
20-year value	$200,960.81
30-year value	$437,383.67
40-year value	$868,174.22
50-year value	$1,653,125.77

$500 Invested Weekly at 9% Compound Interest

Year	Value
1 year value(total value of your account at the end of one year)	$27,182.36
2-year value (total value of your account at the end of two years)	$56,924.61
3-year value (and so on ...)	$89,467.81
4-year value	$125,075.75
5-year value	$164,037.03
10-year value	$421,298.32
15-year value	$824,764.33
20-year value	$1,457,524.99
30-year value	$4,006,231.34
40-year value	$10,275,037.40
50-year value	$25,693,812.29

$500 Invested Weekly at 12% Compound Interest

Year	Value
1-year value (total value of your account at the end of one year)	$27,592.45
2-year value (total value of your account at the end of two years)	$58,702.86
3-year value (and so on ...)	$93,779.74
4-year value	$133,328.82
5-year value	$177,920.28
10-year value	$502,112.19
15-year value	$1,092,828.35
20-year value	$2,169,183.38
30-year value	$7,704,054.66
40-year value	$26,080,474.44
50-year value	$87,092,336.75

Just running these simple examples should be enough of a motivator to get you on the phone to your banker and increase the amount you are contributing to your long-term investments. The power of compounding lies in the duration of the investment. So, when is the very best time to start investing aggressively? When you earn your first paycheck. What is the second best time to start saving and investing aggressively? *Right now!*

7. Sleep on Your Purchases

If you want to be wealthy, you've got to be a master of your emotions. And most impulse purchases are largely a function of emotion rather than logic. So what are your spending habits? What do you say to yourself when you are in the store and being wooed by a luxury item?

You need to become a master of "delayed gratification." This means that you buy things according to your wealth-creation plan as opposed to buying on a whim. However, many people absolutely refuse to delay their gratification; they want things right now. And the conversation they have with themselves might include the following statements:

- It's on sale — look how much money I'd be saving!
- It's the last one on the rack — someone else might buy it if I don't *act now!*
- I've had a bad day, and this purchase will make me happy.
- I've been working hard and I deserve this.
- I just got paid today and I've got lots of cash in the bank.
- My neighbor/brother/co-worker/friend just got one, so I think I should get one too!
- I don't have to pay any money down for a year, but the offer ends today!
- My kids/spouse/parents and I deserve to have the *best.*
- It's a *necessity* — I *have* to have this new car/TV/outfit!

All these thoughts stem from financial immaturity. Most people don't look five minutes into the future to understand that if they don't have the cash to buy something (other than a necessity) then it's usually a bad decision. Financial guru Suze Orman likes to say, "We buy things we don't need to impress people we don't like, with money we don't have."

Try this: don't buy anything on impulse. Nothing. Not a hamburger, not a magazine, not a newspaper, not a soda pop, not a new pair of shoes, not a DVD, not a new cell phone, not a new piece of artwork, not a new living room set, not *anything*. Walk out of the store, go home, and sleep on the purchase. After 24 hours has passed, consider the purchase again. Is it still a burning desire for you? I think you'll find nine times out of ten that your desire has waned. It was a momentary urge, which you managed by walking out of the store. If you still want to buy it, you have to drive back to the store, which is going to cost you time and ultimately money to make the purchase. This is another way to add leverage *against* making the purchase.

I'd recommend that you set aside a certain number of dollars each week for miscellaneous expenses like the ones I've listed. Perhaps you decide that $100 a week fits into your financial plan. So you can blow $100 on anything you want, but once you've used up the $100, no more purchases for the rest of the week! If something is $200, then you have to save this week in order to buy it next week.

Another way of using these impulse purchases to your benefit is to use them as rewards for accomplishing goals. For example, let's say you want to buy a new plasma screen TV. Why don't you set a business goal for yourself, and once you generate a predetermined amount of extra cash on the job, reward yourself with the new TV. That way, your impulse purchases serve to drive the creation of new money, and the extra money created will cover the cost of the purchase.

Dial-In Your Life Partner

Embarking on a transformation journey such as this is going to require more than just straightening out your books and managing your impulse shopping. If you have a significant other who has joined you on your journey through life, you'll want to make sure they're also signed up for your journey to prosperity. One of the greatest challenges that a couple can face in their relationship is when one individual grows faster than the other. If you become exposed to wealth-creating principles and your spouse does not, your enthusiasm may not be relatable.

It is true that money problems are a major cause of divorce in North America. The stress of missed payments, the burden of having to overwork and follow an exhausting schedule, the bitterness of denial and wanting more—these are things that can turn the tender love of a healthy marriage into a battleground about spending habits, priorities and the unanswered dreams of your future. To be successful financially, it is a major asset to have your spouse on-board with your plans—and it can be ruinous to your plans if they oppose.

One of the main factors that causes money tensions in relationships is having differing belief systems when it comes to money. If one person is a saver, believing that we live in a world of scarcity, they will hoard every penny, clip every coupon and live a miserly life. If the second person believes that money is here to create pleasure, then every time they're having a bad day they'll subscribe to the "retail therapy" form of emotional management. One visit to their friend "Nine West" and they're feeling great—with a new pair of $150 shoes to show for it.

As well, your money beliefs control how much money you make, not just what you spend. Most of the time when people complain about money pressure, they are referring to a lack of money. When bills loom large and you have to tighten your belt, one partner may resent the other. After all, if *he* would just make a little more money to close some sales, you could go out to your favorite restaurant more often. And if *she* would just start demanding to be paid what she was worth instead of being taken advantage of by management, your family could afford a nicer house.

Finally, you and your spouse have to agree on how you manage money with the other people in your life. There are many relationships, in addition to that with your life partner, in which money plays an integral factor. If you have children, it is common to want to provide a certain level of lifestyle for them, and you and your partner must agree on what exactly it will entail. Also, aging parents may not have prepared adequately for retirement, or they could be facing healthcare bankruptcy. You and your partner may find yourselves pressed to fund their upkeep. Your wealth may attract attention from extended family as well; if things are going well for you, others may treat you like a bank and expect a little help from time to time. You may feel familial pressure to help out your brother or another family member.

To help you assess your situation, write down thoughtful responses to the following questions:

How does my life partner think and feel about money?
In terms of money, what do we agree on? Disagree on?
What actions have caused financial stress in our relationship?
Which other aspects of our relationship place a strong emphasis on money?

Do I feel obligated to provide financially for others? Why?
What needs to be changed in order to strengthen our finances?
How do I feel about making changes?

Write Your Money Narrative

Just as we have with relationships, with health and with our career, we have a history or "story" with money. Has it been a happy love affair or fraught with anxiety? What have been some of your greatest victories—and greatest disappointments? By identifying our own story, we can start to see some patterns in our current behavior and begin to make changes in our relationship to money today. *We can open our eyes and let the future in!*

Describe a circumstance in which...
You had a triumph with money.
You were "beaten" by money.
You won: a raise, a bonus or a big payday.
You lost.

Where do you want to be in 5, 10, 15, 20, 25, 50 years with money? Rich, comfortable — define it. If doing this feels hard, get over it, and do it anyway.

_____

_____

_____

_____

Who is there with you to accomplish this? Where are you going to get help from? Who wants you to have it as badly as you do?

_____

_____

_____

_____

Often, much of what we learn about money comes from conversations at the family dinner table. For most people, school equipped them with knowledge about algebra and the War of 1812, but very little common sense about how to manage money. Many of our money beliefs have been handed down from our parents, and we adopted them unconsciously.

When you sat around the dinner table, what did you hear? What were the words that people used? Was it all right to talk about money and making money, or was the subject considered taboo in your family?

When someone is born into a rich family, specifically a family where the parents are business owners or business leaders, it is impossible for the children not to be exposed to their parents' beliefs and to be influenced by them. When someone is born into a frugal family, they will be influenced by their parents' behavior. When someone is born into a self-indulgent or wasteful family, they'll emulate those behaviors. When someone is born into a family whose parents have a hard-done-by victim mentality and believe the world didn't give them a fair chance at success, well, they'll likely adopt that bias too.

Consider the following questions and the role they have played in shaping your current financial situation. Are you being held prisoner by the beliefs and strategies of the past? *If so, it's time to rewrite your family's history with money!*

What were your parents' and grandparents' incomes and success levels?
What were their beliefs about money?
What lifestyle did your parents live?
How well did they handle money?

In order to run we must first walk; in order to attract prosperity we must first achieve security and comfort. Mastering the basics of finances creates a powerful foundation that we may use as a springboard toward our greatest dreams. By committing yourself to these principles, you ensure that the doorway toward abundance is open for your ultimate arrival.

Action Steps

What is your *money driver*? Is it security, freedom, or something else? How has having that money driver created blessings in your life—or created challenges? Which money driver do you think would create the greatest blessings? Could you learn to adopt that money driver?

ASSESS YOUR SITUATION. Where are you now? Are you in first gear? Park? Moving toward fifth gear? Are you going in reverse? What can you do this week to begin to move toward the next gear?

1. Set time aside in the next seven days to look over your paperwork and meet with a financial advisor to create a plan that works for you.

TRACK YOUR SPENDING. Don't allow another day to go by without forming this fundamental habit. If you don't know where your money is going, it won't matter if you're making a million dollars a year... if you're spending $1.2 million, you're broke!

2. Get a clear picture of your spending habits by tracking every penny.

MANAGE YOUR MONEY. Do you have any major purchases coming up? How can you best position yourself financially to prepare for those purchases?

3. What can you do this month to make progress on paying down any debts you owe?

Now that we have shifted your financial mindset, it's time to "go for the gold" and create a wealth strategy.

CREATE YOUR WEALTH PLAN

By defining your ultimate vision of your future—your financial destiny, your relationships, your lifestyle, your passions and interests, and the picture of your ideal health—no detail has been left to chance. Through the process of visualization, and by making the conscious choice and subsequent commitment, you can start creating the outcomes that playing the money game will achieve. We are now going to bring all the pieces of the puzzle together and crystallize a specific plan and action steps that will allow you to manifest the wealth you require to live your ultimate life.

Part I: Planning Fundamentals

Just as creating a vision of your ultimate life requires you to apply fundamental goal-setting principles, manifesting wealth draws upon these principles also, but in an even more tangible and strategic way. Developing your strategy to create wealth (what I call your "money game") requires establishing a clear idea of these core elements:

1. The specific, measurable and motivating desired results of your money game
2. The name of your money game
3. Completion date
4. Resources you will need: key players, time required
5. Committed actions
6. Milestones to be reached by end of "the game"
7. Obstacles to overcome
8. Final thoughts:
   a. Where do you need to expand or restore integrity in your financial life — what things must you clear up, communicate, get clear on or get past?
   b. What else needs to be in existence?

Let's discuss each aspect in detail.

WHAT ARE THE SPECIFIC, MEASURABLE AND MOTIVATING OUTCOMES OF YOUR MONEY GAME?

When you achieve success, what will it look like and how much money will you need? For you to win your money game there must be a clearly delineated finish line. Without a checkered flag signaling that you have accomplished your goal, you won't know how near or far away you are from fulfilling your purpose and living your life's mission.

Your outcome must be specific or it will generate inconsistent effort and mixed results. You won't be motivated to push yourself as hard as possible since you won't know where the finish line is. You will reach a point where you feel you've done enough, your effort has yielded results that might be "pretty good" and you feel you are "close enough" to that for which you had hoped. Without a specific goal, you won't know exactly what resources are required of you, whether personal time, investment income, experience or people. The execution of your plan will implode due to not thinking through the resources your outcomes demand and how to acquire them.

As I mentioned in the discussion of what is required to have a Wealth Mastery Mindset, the world admonishes those who have a vague goal and lavishes praise on those who have a specific one. Napoleon Hill clearly articulated that your goal must be *exact*. Precision + clarity = intentionality. So how much money will it take for you to live your life as you desire? $100,000 a year? $500,000? $1 million? $5 million? Will it come from work that you need to repeat or from residual income?

When you know *exactly* what you want and *exactly* what it will take to get it, all your resources are marshaled. All your focus, your energy, your talents and your abilities are brought together to create a focal point that pushes through obstacles, similar to how Napoleon Bonaparte won battle after battle by concentrating his men at the point of attack. Even when outnumbered and outgunned, the force of his battalion bearing down on one point of focus was enough to break the ranks of his opponents and he handily claimed his victories.

When anyone asks you "What is your goal?" you must know the answer without hesitation. For you to achieve massive success in any endeavor, your goal must be at the forefront of your thought. You must know the dream you are chasing and the number of dollars required to attain it. A specific outcome is an amazingly simple yet seemingly rare quality in the planning of most money games. Ensure that your money game is suffused with exactness in its conception, and fill in the following now:

How much money do you require to win your money game and live your life's mission?	
Net Worth:	$_____
Annual Income:	$_____

NAME YOUR MONEY GAME

How do you intend to create the wealth you desire? You've got to create a whole new entity in your life called "wealth creation" or else this activity will get buried under everything else in your schedule and called "life" along with everything else. After reviewing the key principles of wealth creation and several examples of viable money-getting vehicles, what road to prosperity will you choose? Will it be hanging out your own shingle and becoming a highly successful self-employed professional who invests wisely and safely? Will you start your own manufacturing business? Trucking line? Will you get into flipping fixer-upper homes? Purchasing thirty-unit apartment buildings? Buying shopping centers? The possibilities of which money game to choose are limitless, but whichever you choose, it must be named.

Like naming those things that are precious to us, naming "the game" brings it to a level of existence and presence that is larger than if it weren't named. In the context of the money game, are you a Builder, a Banker, a Saver, an Investor, a Risk Taker or a Care Giver? Each name, each "distinction," creates a meaning and purpose that is precise, clear and therefore intentional.

This decision will be determined by several factors, not the least of which is how much capital you currently have and how much you are able to raise through investors. As well, you need to consider your risk threshold: if the business plan doesn't pan out, how much are you willing to lose your first time up to bat? Are you willing to mortgage your home and put your family dwelling up as collateral? Do you need to quit your job in order to run your new business full time and, if so, what will the loss of income do to your family's financial situation? What will the ramifications of that be? What level of trust and commitment do you have from your spouse? Do they support you in the pursuit of your dreams, or do they only have lukewarm enthusiasm for "making it?" What is your level of experience with whatever it is you're pursuing, and how much and how fast are you willing to learn? Do you have experienced advisors on your team who are willing to show you the ropes? How you answer these questions will determine your money game.

Take the example of Jeff Bezos, the billionaire who founded Amazon.com from his garage. Back in 1994, Jeff knew the Internet was taking off and decided to get involved in the gold rush. He knew that people would buy things online but that whatever was sold needed to be something that was easily shipped and wouldn't need to be sampled, tried on in a dressing room or examined up close. After reviewing a list of possible products, he finally settled on books. All the pertinent information about a book, including being able to view pages inside the book and read the back cover, was something that could easily be posted online. Jeff had selected his money game and plunged into the business with vigor, having defined the rules, understood the parameters, mastered the plays and generated a score he could live for and live with. It was a game that would move, touch and empower him.

> What is your Money Game? In what way are you going to create wealth? For example, what business will you create?
>
> _____
>
> _____
>
> _____
>
> _____
>
> _____

WHAT IS YOUR COMPLETION DATE?

On the rare occasions that people set goals, one of the primary reasons they don't accomplish the goal is that they don't have a completion date set in concrete. Without a deadline we aren't motivated to take action. The distractions of things that seem important tend to overtake the focus of long-term objectives, and we risk devolving into a person who is busy doing unimportant things. Consequently, the competitors that challenge us in life can divert us in the race to success. These competitors don't need to be people; we are in competition against our aging bodies, against circumstance and disaster, against atrophy in our relationships and against market trends over which we have no control. Interestingly, the greatest competitor that we face is ourselves: our weaknesses, our fears, our procrastination and our indulgences.

A deadline forces us to look past our emotions for the sake of a long-term vision of excellence. We may recognize our emotions, but we treat them as an interesting afterthought, much like we would treat the weather as a minor distraction and not worthy of much attention. We know that there is work to be done, regardless of whether we are tired, hungry, lonely, scared, discouraged or lazy. Champions don't make decisions based upon whether they *feel* like doing something; they make decisions based upon whether a decision aligns with their long-term goals.

Left to their own devices, even the greatest champions may struggle to mobilize themselves on a daily basis if they don't have a target date for completion within their crosshairs. Without a target date, we have no perspective on whether a goal is near term or long term; an immediate payoff or a larger return down the road. This also impacts incentive.

Ever notice that things that expire are used sooner? For example, perishable goods like dairy products, medication and food. Things with a clearly stated life span are consumed, used up and taken seriously — or else lost. Our completion date is like an expiry date: the purpose is to get done what we must by a specific date, because when we don't, our right to celebrate is hindered.

A completion date also mobilizes our customers and our colleagues. When a new operating system is about to be launched, computer dealers and software developers build their business initiatives around the product launch. When Hollywood studios announce the release date of a tent-pole summer popcorn flick, an entire army of marketing geniuses coordinates its efforts to ensure all the theater seats are filled on opening night. When real estate developers announce a completion date for construction, dozens of families organize their lives around the moving day schedule. A specific completion date is a fundamental piece of your success puzzle. Record yours here:

By what DATE will you reach your money goal?

WHAT RESOURCES WILL YOU REQUIRE?

As you prepare to embark on your journey toward prosperity, you will need to identify and assemble the requisite resources to make your trip a success. Crossing the vast chasm between the status quo and massive success will require a commensurate level of preparation and resources. Climbing the bleachers at your university requires merely the desire; climbing Mount Everest requires a small army and years of planning.

There are several key resources that your journey will require:

- Time
- Information
- Capital
- Teammates
- Connections
- Experience and Training

Time

If you wish to stifle your business at the point of conception, simply ignore it. If you want a quantifiable measurement to gauge your potential success, you need look no further than your calendar. As much as a person may profess to the contrary, whatever you value finds its way into your schedule. If you say you value exercise but never find the time, you haven't made it a priority. If you say you value your kids but are never home, they aren't at the top of your list. If you value the success of your money-making venture, you will clearly delineate the hours of your day that you will invest in growing your wealth.

Information

In war, the army with the greatest communication skills will dominate the battlefield. Ancient Middle Eastern armies would dominate their opponents by the skillful raising of tall flags that directed the troops with words such as "attack," "regroup," "archers," "foot soldiers," and so forth. The men up and down the lines could see the flags and knew what to do. In business, whoever has the most information will be able to take advantage of market trends and skillfully negotiate any deal more successfully.

For example, if you know that you are negotiating with someone who is at a point of desperation, whether due to slowing sales, increased rent or late shipments, that information can be used to your tactical advantage. The strongest position in a negotiation is always when you are able to walk away from the deal and you know that the other person doesn't have that option. If you know that the guy across the table has to close the deal by June 1 and you stall things until May 29, you might find that he suddenly becomes much more flexible on his terms if he can't find someone else to sell to.

As well, if you have information about emerging market trends, you will be well positioned to capitalize on them. What is common knowledge to the average person today was being discussed in high-level meetings several years ago. Being able to spot the next big thing and drive a wave of success is one of the critical components of massive financial success. It's no good to realize when it's too late, things like, "If only I'd invested in Microsoft when it was just getting started! Or Walmart!" Successfully investing in emerging companies requires that you have full command of the trends before the information becomes common knowledge.

Starbucks Chairman and CEO Howard Schultz built his business by recognizing emerging trends. He was a VP for a Swedish housewares company when he noticed that a little business in Seattle was placing a lot of orders for a special type of coffeemaker. Intrigued, Schultz visited this emerging coffee business and met with the owners. He immediately saw the potential in their philosophy of offering high-quality coffee beans from around the world and their commitment to product excellence. At the time, they were in the business of selling coffee beans to connoisseurs. Schultz lobbied for a year to become a partner and co-owner in the fledgling company. His second insight occurred on a trip to Italy, where he visited numerous espresso bars and studied what made them special. He watched the flamboyant people who served the coffee, noting that they were called "baristas," and observed how much the customers enjoyed their coffee and the setting. He saw the socializing and sense of community, and he realized that this was what he needed to bring back to America. By having the vision to transform his coffeehouse into a customer experience, Howard Schultz built Starbucks into the iconic American business it is today.

Capital

According to the US Bureau of Labor Statistics, only 44 percent of new businesses are still operating successfully after the first four years.[4] One of the primary reasons for business failure is lack of

4 http://www.bls.gov/opub/mir/2005/05/ressum.pdf

capital to keep the doors open. Most good ideas are underfunded, meaning that the business owner doesn't have the money to pay rent on their retail space, to advertise effectively to build a client base, or to purchase the right equipment and infrastructure to manage their growing business. Moreover, they don't have the money to expand in order to keep up with demand. The two biggest reasons for not having enough capital are:

1. the inability to raise venture capital, and
2. poor forecasting and unrealistic budgets that don't take emergencies into account.

If you can't raise venture capital, you either need very deep pockets personally (which raises the question: Where did your money come from in the first place?) or you had better partner with someone who is very skilled at sales and raising venture capital. If you don't speak enthusiastically to investors about your idea, why would anyone get excited? People invest in someone who is passionate and confident in their idea. And if you expect to sell your product or service to customers, you need to be good at sales. Being good at sales is almost a prerequisite of business success.

Consider that capital can also come in the form of assistance or sponsorship. In-kind contributions can be granted, given or donated to you in the form of supplies, manpower, volunteers, consulting—just about anything. The key is that when you're looking for capital or assistance, you have to know that people are looking for three things: 1) a clear purpose for the money; 2) a solid tracking system and the integrity to track and account for each and every expense; and 3) a commitment from you to put your own money and resources into the venture first.

Teammates

I can't imagine myself not having a strong business team playing the money game with me. I am truly blessed to be surrounded by such high-quality people. I have an efficient and engaged team in my office who support me and make me more effective by managing the daily administration of my businesses, and because I come up with ideas faster than I can implement them, it's great to have people who can execute the projects that I envision or initiate. I also have a cadre of trusted advisors, tax attorneys, lawyers, accountants and mentors whom I call upon for advice, wisdom and sometimes merely to serve as a sounding board for my grandiose schemes. My advisors keep me grounded, catch the details that I miss and add their creativity to solving business problems that we face.

Connections

The great Tony Robbins says, "Proximity is power." Stick around the people who are making the deals and you will be closer to the action when it goes down. You will meet the brightest and the best and learn from them. If you want to get into the music business, hang around successful musicians. If you want to get into sports, hang around successful athletes. If you want to make money, hang around successful millionaires.

I have a personal story that is a great example of what Robbins preaches on the magic and power of "proximity." I used to be an attendee at Power Within events just like anyone else, until I began paying a sponsorship fee to have a booth at the shows. Slowly I negotiated for the rights to distribute free giveaways and then seat drops (free gifts on each seat, ensuring that all attendees knew I was there). This led eventually to my developing a relationship with the promoter, and I built up his comfort and confidence in me to begin introducing keynote speakers. I introduced speakers including Tony Robbins himself, as well as Bill Clinton, Sir Richard Branson,

Christopher Gardner, Suze Orman, Bob Proctor, Jack Canfield and Harvey Mackay, to name a few.

Because of the power of proximity, it is no coincidence that many of my endorsements have come from the very people I have not only introduced, but with whom I now share the stage as an accomplished author and speaker. I was there by choice, by design — on purpose.

Traveling in entrepreneurial circles exposes you to more and more business opportunities. While average people are talking about the baseball game on the weekend, successful entrepreneurs are talking about the next deal. Because of this, the more you build your network, the more conversations you have, and therefore the more the deals will land in your lap. Famous American investor Robert Kiyosaki refers to this as "deal flow." You want to be exposed to as many deals as possible so that you have more to choose from and can pick the winners. Being exposed to more deals gives you the insight to discern whether you are looking at a lemon or a cash cow.

Connections also open doors to resources. For example, you may need to hire a key player and one of your golfing buddies knows just the person to head up your new marketing department. You may need to manufacture a new product and one of your best friends has a college buddy who is looking to sell his manufacturing plant, and your business would keep the doors open. You may want to import a product from another country but don't speak the language and don't know anyone on the ground; your bilingual cousin studied overseas and worked for a wholesaler who is looking to get rid of the excess product that isn't selling in their market. Connections abound in every conversation, with every person you meet. Become a collector of human potential and talent, and seemingly impassable obstacles will magically disappear.

Experience and Training

Don't be intimidated if you know nothing about the product that you'd like to sell or the service or industry in which you'd like to get involved. People don't make money focusing on the reasons why something won't be easy; they get rich by being creative and finding a way. It's always preferable to focus on your area of expertise, but if an amazing opportunity comes along in an area that you know nothing about, go for it! Never let a lack of experience or inside knowledge overshadow your enthusiasm.

If you don't have experience in an area that is a necessity for your business success, you must resolve to master that area — or, at the very least, obtain a level of functional competence. In fact, I'd go so far as to say that you should always strive to develop your strengths and have a maintenance level of skill in your areas of weakness. *If you choose to focus on your natural weaknesses, you will simply develop very strong weaknesses.*

Speaking from my own experience, I encourage you to do what Tony Robbins preaches: find the very best people in whatever it is you wish to do, and mirror them. Since the 1990s, I have sought relationships with some of North America's top thinkers and leaders inside the wealth management industry and I've been able to work by their side for months and, in some cases, years. As I was earning millions of dollars, and responsible collectively for billions, I learned firsthand and matured in their ethos of success — everything there was to know about running a powerful and purposeful financial practice.

I did not graduate from high school, let alone attend university. I received no formal training in speaking, nor in business or money management. I did, however, become a ferocious student of life, reading a book a week, underlining anything that was worth noting, taking classes, studying speakers, being willing to be inspired and being committed to regenerating the same level of verve — on purpose.

So I encourage you to become a voracious learner and be committed to continuous self-improvement. Seek out and hire experts in the areas of your weakness, and learn enough to understand what they advise you on and why their opinions are valid.

Describe the **RESOURCES** you will require to accomplish your goals:

Time _____

Information _____

Capital _____

Teammates _____

Connections _____

Experience
and Training _____

_____

_____

COMMITTING TO AND MOBILIZING YOUR PLAN

Launching a successful enterprise is like composing a symphony: each section must be organized to work in harmony with the other. When one section is ignored, the result can be unpleasant or even disastrous. With something as complicated as a business, made up of its multitude of moving parts (relationships, products, marketing, infrastructure, vendors, technology, capital support, etc.), it's easy to see why many businesses don't recoup their initial investment and fade from view within a short few years.

In designing your plan for wealth, you will need to break down your major goals into bite-size pieces, ready for immediate execution. When we have a checklist of accomplishments to achieve we are more apt to measure and record daily progress. As well, when we stumble it is much easier to do a "post-mortem" and identify where the error occurred: what was missed at the planning stage, what was executed sloppily or what was executed perfectly but planned poorly.

Planning each step in advance allows you to spot costly errors while they are still just ideas on paper. It gives your mastermind team and your mentor something tangible to digest and offer consultation on. As well, when you promise these actions in writing to your team members and your mentor, you now have the extra motivation of keeping your word. It is now a matter of public record that you intend to follow through with your written plan. Fear, laziness and indecisiveness are now in conflict with your integrity, for you have the added pressure of wanting to keep your promise to the people you respect and admire.

Brainstorm every necessary step required to launch your venture, and as you design your plan be sure to make your plans a public declaration of action. What might be some of the steps on your journey to wealth creation? Perhaps you will:

- Conduct focus groups to develop and customize products
- Research your competitors and learn what they are doing right and what to avoid
- Raise $1 million in venture capital in ninety days
- Prepare your marketing strategy
- Design an org chart and hire a headhunter to identify candidates for key roles on your team
- Create a budget
- Create a list of required assets: buildings, furniture, telecommunications equipment, computers, materials, etc.
- Make five new business contacts each day
- Make fifty cold calls to prospective clients each day

Whatever the steps might be, your promise to your mastermind team and mentors is a powerful tool to fully mobilize your efforts! Now that you have determined what actions you must take, you must next determine the deadline for each of these actions. You must designate milestones to be accomplished along your journey to success.

What ACTIONS will you consider and commit to?	By what date?
1. _____	_____
2. _____	_____
3. _____	_____
4. _____	_____
5. _____	_____

REACHING YOUR MILESTONES

In 1961, President John F. Kennedy stood before an audience at Rice University and proclaimed to the world that the United States would land a man on the moon by the end of the decade. Kennedy's lead rocket scientist was a German by the name of Dr. Wernher von Braun—who was stunned to hear the proclamation. He knew how far the American space program needed to advance its technology in order to accomplish the seemingly impossible task of putting a man in orbit around the earth and successfully bringing him home alive. They would need to develop a landing craft that could bring the astronauts safely to the moon's surface and then lift off again into orbit. Once in the moon's orbit, the landing module would need to reconnect with the main module in orbit around the moon.

But before any of that could be accomplished, they needed to create liquid rocket fuel that would allow the main rocket to break free of the earth's gravity. The problem with solid-state fuel is that its own weight figures into the equation; the heavier the rocket, the more fuel you need to lift it, which increases the weight, which in turn increases the need to fuel — a serious problem indeed. Dr. von Braun reasoned that if they could accomplish the first milestone of developing liquid rocket fuel that would allow them to put a man in orbit around Earth, they were on the path to putting a man on the moon by the end of the decade. Once they had accomplished this first milestone, it would create momentum in the space program and belief that the final objective could be completed.

As the old saying goes, the way to eat an elephant is one bite at a time. If the scientists were to focus solely on the end goal of putting a man on the moon, it would seem too far away; they wouldn't have the belief or motivation to do the seemingly impossible. But by creating specific milestones that edged them closer and closer to the ultimate objective, NASA reached its goal. It all began by breaking the objective down into bite-size, achievable milestones.

This parallels any successful enterprise. If you are a land developer, you need to have an architect draw up the plans for the homes, get the proper zoning permits to build, create a successful sales and marketing initiative targeting prospective buyers, break ground, lay the foundation, put up the frames and then add the electrical, plumbing, drywall, carpet, paint, brick exterior and the final finishing touches. Each one of these stages builds upon the next.

For you to be successful in your money game, you would do well to break down your journey into realistic milestones. If you are opening a retail outlet, some of the milestones along your journey may include researching your market, assembling a core team of partners, developing your marketing plans, raising venture capital, selecting an advantageous location, negotiating with vendors, setting up your office, hiring staff, ordering product, launching your marketing campaign, planning a huge promotional event for your launch day, driving sales to meet your profit objectives, franchising your concept and opening additional locations.

OVERCOMING YOUR OBSTACLES

In preparing for our journey, it's important to pause and consider the challenges that we may face along the road. Challenges that may have been easily overcome with preparation can be exacerbated when they catch us off guard. The great voyageurs of history depended upon their telescopes to spot rough terrain or stormy weather ahead at sea. Our foresight, creativity, experience and the wisdom of our mentors can serve as a metaphorical telescope to help us traverse any rocky terrain we may face.

Consider the obstacles that you have faced in previous adventures. Like all people, you have no doubt missed achieving a goal that you had set your sights on. What caused you to miss the goal? Did you run out of time and money, energy, or the support of your team? Did you face injury to your body or to your business? Did you face a disaster that was seemingly inconceivable, such as a medical emergency, an act of Mother Nature, or a sudden shortage of a critical component in the manufacturing process? Did you deal with a vendor who did not honor their commitment to you? Did you face dissension within the ranks, stock shrinkage due to employee theft, or betrayal by a loved one?

While it is certainly difficult to anticipate every obstacle that we may face, there are several ways to increase our chances of doing so. First, we can learn from past challenges and proactively establish procedures and processes to ensure that history does not repeat itself. Secondly, we can brainstorm with our trusted team of advisers about potential challenges that we have not yet considered. One of the great values in having a mastermind team and/or a mentor is that they may be able to spot obstacles before we do. Schedule brainstorming sessions to identify potential problems and develop a plan to ward them off.

As strange as this may seem, it can also help to have someone who is slightly pessimistic evaluate your business plan. Although I don't recommend associating with negative people, their perspective may serve as the proverbial canary in the coal mine to spot potential problems that someone with a more optimistic viewpoint may overlook.

In the worksheet below, consider what obstacles you might face. What areas will these obstacles fall under? Describe the potential obstacle, and then in the space that follows describe in a few words how you might prepare for and ultimately prevent this challenge from throwing you off track. I've filled in a few examples for you.

What OBSTACLES might you face — and how might you plan to OVERCOME them?		
Area	Obstacle	Potential Solution
Sales	Not generating enough leads	Develop promotion to attract new clients
Personal Income	Not generating enough cash flow	Develop another strategy to solve issue

Questions for Reflection

In preparation for your journey, answering the following questions will help to create space so that your future is open and ready to accept prosperity.

Where do I need to expand or restore integrity in my financial life — what things must I clear up, communicate, get clear on or get past?

Unfinished business in the realm of integrity will leave a cloud of negativity over all your dealings. If the word on the street is that you're not scrupulous, you may need to take time to renew faith in your good name before a successful enterprise can be launched.

A break with integrity may also be that you have not been honoring your promises to yourself. If you've given up on a goal before, you may need to restore your own faith in your ability to follow through and complete the task at hand.

What else needs to be in existence?

This final question is the safety net in case anything has been missed in the preparation process. With such an open-ended question, it allows us a rare moment of introspection to look inside and see if there are any internal conflicts that may still be holding us back from enjoying the success that we crave. You may have forecasted sales figures and stock levels, assembled a team of competent marketing professionals and enthusiastically raised venture capital for your idea. Despite all that, sometimes the "something else" that needs to be in existence is a sense of inner peace that everything is going to be okay.

Perhaps what needs to be in existence is acceptance that it's okay to have failed before, because today we choose to rise again. Perhaps what needs to be in existence is forgiveness of those who have betrayed or hurt us in the past. Whatever it may be, look past the charts and figures and search deep inside yourself to learn if there are any final variables unstated in your formula for success.

Part II: Wealth Strategies

THE POWER OF COMPOUNDING: 1 PERCENT OF 100 PEOPLE

J. Paul Getty, author of *How to Be Rich* and one of the great oil tycoons at the turn of the 20th century, famously said, "I'd rather have 1 percent of the effort of 100 men than 100 percent of my own."

In creating wealth, we would be wise to remember that time is one resource that is fixed. With only twenty-four hours in which to operate, we have three choices. We can work more hours for the same wage, which will create an incremental increase in our salary. We can dramatically increase our hourly wage, which will create comfort. Or we can get paid for the efforts of many people, which will create wealth.

Consider any self-employed professional who has built a successful six-figure career. This individual is likely to be stuck on a treadmill, as they have likely upgraded their lifestyle due to their increased income. They can't stop working, and so each day they must get back on the treadmill to begin the race again. Because they must now sustain that lifestyle, they can't get sick or take a vacation without suffering from the loss of income.

Now, take any profession and leverage it. Consider a successful real-estate salesman who trains ten other people to successfully sell real estate under his marquee and using the credibility of his the branding and advertising materials. In return, he receives a percentage of their sales, perhaps 10 percent. Now the professional is no longer limited to his own efforts; he can increase his business at will.

The same example could be applied to a doctor who owns a medical building and has a team of doctors, a fitness trainer who opens a gym, a piano teacher who opens a music school, or a carpenter who opens a home-framing business. Whatever you do professionally, look for ways to leverage your profession and get a percentage of the efforts of many people instead of 100 percent of only your own effort.

The great challenge for professionals to overcome is the challenge of delegation. You understand that you could personally close the real-estate sale, train the fitness client or diagnose the patient more effectively than your counterparts. Perhaps they are only at 80 percent of your level of expertise and you feel frustrated with their performance. Leveraging yourself requires that you become satisfied with the good performance of people on your team. Perfectionism should be used as a tool to improve quality rather than an obstacle to achieving greater goals.

As well, the moment you assemble a team of people, you become the de facto leader of that team; however, being successful at your profession does not automatically engender leadership ability in you. You'll also need to set up administration systems and support for members of your team in order for your business to function efficiently. These might be tasks that would be better suited to an administrative assistant, which requires further investments. With a small team the extra investment in time and money may not seem as great as the financial reward. So you have to decide how big your team needs to be in order to be a viable business option.

OWN YOUR OWN BUSINESS

As long as you work for other people you will be paid what a company determines your job is worth. If you are in a salaried position your income may not be affected by your overtime. Any dramatic increases in your pay will be at the discretion of the person who signs your paycheck. If you want a raise, you have to ask their permission. If you want to take time off, you have to ask their permission. Ultimately, your life is not completely in your control.

Even so, many people choose to stay in a job because of the illusion of security. Most people rank security as one of their highest needs, with financial security often at the absolute top of the list. People mistakenly believe that if they have a paycheck, they have security; people face an uncomfortable education about security if their company goes through a round of layoffs or, worse, business failure and bankruptcy.

Having your own business gives you much greater control of your life. You determine your value. You work on projects that you are passionate about. You work as hard as you want and charge as much as you want. You assemble a team that you work well with. Office politics, favoritism and cronyism are a thing of the past when you are the owner.

As well, you enjoy tax benefits when you are a business owner. One of the great keys to maximizing wealth is to reduce your taxes and reinvest the tax savings. Hiring a brilliant tax attorney and accountant are key strategies to maximizing these benefits.

CREATE A BUSINESS SYSTEM
One key difference between being self-employed and being a massive business owner is whether or not you can walk away from your business and have it still operating profitably without your presence. A lot of people who own a business do not have a business system that gives them freedom; they are simply self-employed professionals with an office and support staff who allow them to be more effective and profitable. As soon as the business owner leaves for vacation, the business loses its magic.

Ray Kroc was a successful milkshake salesman in the 1950s when he noticed a large number of orders coming from a particular restaurant located in California. He decided to visit the flourishing burger restaurant, which was owned by two brothers, Dick and Mac McDonald. Kroc immediately realized the potential in the business and wanted to go into business with the brothers. When he asked them how big they saw the business growing, they felt that perhaps they could add a few more stores. Kroc partnered with them and eventually bought them out.

He had realized that the McDonald brothers did not understand the power of a business system. In order for an enterprise to grow exponentially, it must be replicable. They needed to create a turnkey enterprise that franchisees could, in turn, open across the country. Instead of opening a few stores, they could open thousands and reap massive financial benefits. Kroc went to work building what would become McDonald's Hamburger University, a training facility for franchise managers and owner/operators. For years, he did not take a salary, instead reinvesting every penny back into his company. He gathered together the key managers to discuss what ideas were working, further refining his business system.

Today, when you walk into any McDonald's restaurant, you will have the same experience that a McDonald's customer is having elsewhere in your country and even elsewhere in the world. There is almost no limit to how many McDonald's restaurants can be operated successfully across the globe.

If you are going to create massive wealth, ask yourself if your business is readily scalable. Is it dependent on you, or can it be replicated over and over with a turnkey business system that removes you from the equation? Remember that if you can't be replaced in life, you can't be promoted in life.

SPOT THE EMERGING TRENDS

If we are to create massive wealth in our lives, spotting trends—and even creating them—will be a critical component of our success. Paul Zane Pilzer, author of *Unlimited Wealth*, points out that the majority of the things we spend money on today did not exist ten years ago. It stands to reason that ten years from now, a good deal of the money we spend will be on products and services that do not yet exist today. While there may be no *need* for these futuristic products and services, some enterprising and creative entrepreneurs will bring into existence things that people feel they absolutely cannot live without.

To capture a market, it can sometimes be easiest to simply create the market and be the leader at the forefront. In fact, so many examples of companies who have captured the market can be seen in our ubiquitous use of the product name that dominates the market and now stands in for the generic name. For example, we say "google it" instead of "look it up," Kleenex instead of facial tissue, McNuggets instead of chicken nuggets, Jacuzzi instead of hot tub, and so on.

Below are a few examples of products and services that were created in response to needs that their founders intuited through careful study of trends in human behavior, changing social norms and of course personal and business technology. As a result of creating and meeting huge market demand for their products, their founders have reaped huge fortunes.

- Facebook, Twitter, LinkedIn and other social media came on the scene in 2004 in response to the need for people to connect — either by re-establishing connections from their past or by connecting people with common interests. These online forums are still relatively new, yet they are now as familiar — and as necessary — to their millions of users as the air they breathe. Mark Zuckerberg, founder and CEO of Facebook, is worth some $28 billion, according to *Forbes* in 2014.
- Needing to record the high points of our lives through photography, whether from the top of a wave or the top of a mountain, was the inspiration behind GoPro, the compact, wearable, waterproof, professional-quality

video camera. Since launching the product in 2004 and building the brand through various iterations, GoPro creator Nick Woodman has caused a revolution in the world of extreme sports, brought a game-changer to the way Hollywood films are made, and amassed a net worth of almost $1.4 billion.

- With so many competing and incompatible mobile messaging devices on the market, Jan Koum saw the need for a smartphone app that could let everyone get along. WhatsApp Messenger is a cross-platform mobile messaging app that allows users to exchange messages without having to pay for SMS. Koum sold the business to Facebook in 2014, for $19 billion in stock and cash.

- Drew Houston is another young billionaire who helped fill a need before we knew we had it. One of the co-founders of Dropbox, a cloud-based file-sharing service created in 2007, Houston is now worth approximately $1.2 billion.

Don't just focus on technology, though. Let demographic trends and social trends guide you in finding and creating your market niche. For example, the baby boomers are retiring by the millions as I write this. Through the last sixty years, whatever age this generation was, the companies that created products for that age group would flourish. When the baby boomers were first born, the companies Pampers and Gerber flourished. As those same boomers are entering retirement, products and services aimed at the senior generation are enjoying great success.

There is also a worldwide focus on environmentalism that has surged in recent years. Products and services that have natural and organic ingredients, or offer other earth-friendly benefits, will capitalize on this trend — a trend that shows no sign of slowing down.

To be at the forefront, like the examples above, you'll need to be an astute student of technological and social trends.

HELP ENOUGH PEOPLE GET WHAT THEY WANT ...

Earlier I quoted Zig Ziglar, the motivational speaker and author who famously says, "Help enough people get what they want and you will get what you want." The question then becomes, "What do people want?"

While many companies exhaust their time and money guessing at the answer to this question, launching ill-conceived products that sit unpurchased on retail shelves and consuming millions of advertising dollars, Dell does the opposite. Instead of spending a great deal of time trying to guess what consumers want, Michael Dell simply asks them. Since founding the Dell Computer Corporation from his university dorm room in 1984, he has expanded it into a multi-billion-dollar empire. After making his company private in 2013, *Forbes* listed his net worth at $22.3 billion.[5]

What makes Dell unique is that he does not dictate to the customer what products he will offer; in fact, every product is completely customizable. Through online surveys and customer focus groups, Dell researches the basic structure of computers that are in demand for all his customer groups and then lets people pick and choose their preferred features.[6]

Dell brilliantly assembles his business segments around his customers, grouping them according to the categories consumer, different business sizes and government. You'll never find a Dell computer waiting on a shelf ready to be shipped; every computer is assembled from scratch once the order has arrived. At the same time, an order is placed with the supplier to manufacture and ship the parts required.

Consider the incredible value this process offers. With no inventory collecting dust on a shelf and tying up capital resources, Dell is able to reduce costs and pass the savings on to customers. Remaining in the black has never been easier. With such a

5 http://www.forbes.com
6 Krames, Jeffery A. *What the Best CEOs Know* (McGraw-Hill, 2005, p.27)

customer-centric model, it revolutionizes the traditional model of walking into a computer shop and simply buying off the shelf what the store told you was available. As well, Dell's goal is to have 100 percent of his sales take place over the Internet, with no intervening interaction between human beings; your computer interfaces with their computer and the transaction is seamless. If you want an extra DVD burner, you just order one and the computer arrives with it installed. More automation means a smaller overall payroll, which translates to additional savings. Dell stays relevant in the marketplace by allowing customization and listening to what his customers want, and he is a billionaire because of it.

Part III: Building Your Mastermind Team

CREATING AND LIVING INSIDE YOUR SPECIALIZED SPHERE OF INFLUENCE

Robert Kiyosaki, author of *Rich Dad, Poor Dad*, says that our income is an average of the incomes of the five people we spend the most time with. Who are you spending time with? If you want to estimate what your income will be five years from now, do this simple exercise using Kiyosaki's formula.

Napoleon Hill was an equally staunch proponent of the concept of positive association. He implored students of success to form a "mastermind group" of associates who assemble for the purpose of encouragement, problem solving, personal improvement, networking and leveraging each other's resources. These resources might be connections, money, or time and energy.

In 1727, Benjamin Franklin assembled twelve of his closest friends and created the Junto Society. This was an organization of scholarly associates, businessmen and high achievers who would meet each week to discuss philosophy, business and success. They would read great works of literature, discuss market trends and politics, and give reports and presentations on what they had discovered that week, all of which was geared toward the improvement of each of the members. These meetings continued after Franklin's death and evolved into what it is now called the American Philosophical Society.

Think about the team you would bring together as your mastermind group or Junto Society. How could your team move your business and life forward? What traits and characteristics would the team members bring to the table? I would recommend that you select high achievers, and in particular look for people who have surpassed you in an arena that you wish to master. You want innovators on your team, as well as mentors and coaches.

Take a moment and consider your ultimate dream team. You may be able to create new relationships and invite them to be part of your own Junto Society. Out of your current network of established relationships, what key people would you select that you believe would be equally committed to self-improvement and be dedicated to meeting on a regularly scheduled basis? Write their names down now:

Your MASTERMIND TEAM	
Name	Area of Expertise
1. _____	_____
2. _____	_____
3. _____	_____
4. _____	_____
5. _____	_____

Steel sharpens steel, and only a strong mastermind team will provide the benefits described above. The people we associate with, we in many ways become. Therefore, treat the promotion to your inner circle as the doorway to a priceless vault that guards your greatest treasure; only the cherished few who hold themselves to the highest standards may be allowed to pass.

Part IV: Mentorship

I am very fortunate and grateful to have been mentored by the likes of a former Navy SEALs commander, as well as personal transformation masters, leading platform presenters and champions of philanthropy—a number of highly professional, disciplined and committed human beings that stand as champions for being excellent.

The mentors I have been blessed to have had in my life truly are, collectively, responsible for the genetic code of my existence. I am a better man for having read books and works by Tony Robbins, Werner Erhard, Napoleon Hill, Jean-Paul Sartre, Martin Heidegger and many more. If I were to make a list of the people whom I respect and emulate, and what I learned from them, this list would include: Mr. Costello, who showed me how to present with power; Mr. Allen, who taught me the arts of visualization and business management; Mr. Panzures, who inspired me to work harder than imaginable; Mr. Deasley, who showed me how to live larger than life; Dr. Stoltz, who gave me the quality of resilience; Ms. Robinson, who taught me to own myself; Mr. Corey, who instilled in me the value of impeccability and playing full out; Mr. Town, who taught me how "big equals billions"; and my dear friend Mr. Khoja, who's given me my work ethic of "getting it done" and generating memorable moments for all people.

This is not merely a list of shout-outs. These are the people who contributed greatly to who I am. I can't imagine what I would be doing for a living if it hadn't been for them. Imagine your life without your list of mentors. And if you have none to list, consider whether it's perhaps because you're not allowing yourself to be vulnerable enough or not playing large enough to allow someone to contribute to you in a way that is irreversibly positive.

Two magical things happen in the experience of mentorship: first, you are forever transformed by having been contributed to; and second, the mentor is transformed for having given a piece of themselves away. Even masters who channel their craft into great works have mentors and advisors to direct their growth and progress. Beethoven studied under Joseph Haydn; Aristotle studied under Plato; Alexander the Great was tutored by Aristotle. Mentorship molds the greatness that resides within you and maximizes your efforts in the right direction. I'm going to share some key principles on the relationship that you must have with your mentor, and how you should value that relationship. These principles have guided me successfully:

The mentor's experience and expertise will help you:
- see obstacles in your path
- save time
- push you to be your best

You must understand that a mentor:
- must be pursued
- will offer you his or her time, which must be cherished
- may focus on only one area
- may answer only what you ask

I'll now delve a little deeper into each of these, to give you a clearer sense of how invaluable a mentor can be in assisting you on your journey to achieving the wealth you desire.

A Mentor Will See Obstacles in Your Path

Mentors have already scaled the heights that you are now attempting. Their vantage point on the other side of success affords them an aerial view of your landscape; they can see that forty paces ahead on the mountain path there lies a boulder and so they are able to direct you to change course. It is up to you to be humble enough to accept their direction. Because they have encountered many more situations than you, they have created many more answers to those situations; they have a formidable toolbox of options to deal with the many variables on your journey.

A Mentor Will Save You Time

The wisdom a mentor possesses has been hard-won through times of great challenge, failure and ultimately success. You can obtain the same wisdom in one of two ways: invest your irreplaceable time and suffer through trial and error, or absorb a mentor's biography and glean the lessons from the pages of their life. The most efficient way to gain experience is to learn through the experiences of others. Just as it is wise to follow in the footsteps of another person while crossing a minefield, it is wise to follow in the footsteps of a mentor who has accomplished what you seek. As Sir Isaac Newton wrote, "If I have been able to see farther than others, it is because I stood on the shoulders of giants."

A Mentor Will Push You To Be Your Best

Friends and family may be forgiving of mistakes and half-hearted efforts; a true mentor is not. Because a mentor has accomplished what you seek, they know that the goal is attainable if the appropriate effort, growth and commitment are applied. Because of this, mentors are less tolerant of excuses. A mentor knows what is possible. A mentor sees what you are capable of. A mentor sees past the emotion of the moment and knows that you can do more. A mentor knows when you are giving up too soon and, conversely, when you have exhausted yourself in your effort. A mentor holds you accountable to the promises you make; you must complete the task at hand or risk losing their respect. A mentor helps you to become the greatest version of yourself possible.

A Mentor Must Be Pursued

Everything of value must be pursued; rarely, if ever, does it fall accidentally into our lap. Love, wealth, health and happiness are capricious elements that must be wooed and maintained with diligent effort if their presence in your life is to be assured. The same is true of great mentors. You must prove to them that you are worthy of their investment in you. Great people know their own value and the value of their time. If you are to be their apprentice, you must seek out the mentor, not the other way around. A true mentor does not assign themselves the title, just as a true visionary does not promote themselves as such. Only the apprentice can identify someone as a mentor, and then you must make a case as to why they should invest in you. Often, a mentor expects nothing more than your appreciation and the earnest application of their wisdom. They expect you to follow their advice — that is the price of admission and how to honor such a cherished connection. To ignore the advice of the mentor is to say "I don't respect you," which is unacceptable, as every great mentor holds respect as a fundamental value.

A Mentor's Time Must Be Cherished

As time is the one commodity that can never be replenished, the greatest gift that a human being can offer another is the gift of their time. If you have made it onto your mentor's calendar, you are most fortunate. Every moment in the presence of your mentor should be treasured. Always arrive early so that you are able to start the meeting on time; wait outside if you must and read a book or review your past notes from discussions with your mentor. Always have a notepad, pen, laptop or digital audio recorder ready to take down notes; unless your memory is perfect, you will want to capture the nuggets of wisdom that your mentor is sharing. Furthermore, not taking notes suggests that what your mentor is sharing is not worth remembering. You don't have to be feverishly scribbling down every word they say, because that might be equally distracting for them. Simply ask at the beginning of the meeting if you have their permission to take notes or even record the discussion.

A Mentor May Focus on Only One Area

It is realistic that you may have several mentors, each offering wisdom and guidance in a key area of life. One mentor may offer wisdom on the subject of integrity and ethical behavior, while another may specialize in peak physical fitness. Another mentor may guide you in the realm of spiritual understanding and faith, and an additional mentor may be a genius at creating wealth and living an abundant life. It is not necessary for a mentor to be successful in every area for them to offer value. Therefore, you may need to seek out several mentors who specialize in the areas of your interest. It is unwise to tear down a mentor because of failure in one area; it is fantasy to imagine that one person has achieved perfection in all arenas. A mentor may have great courage on the battlefield, yet may struggle with fidelity in their marriage. A mentor may have great personal wealth, yet is physically unfit. Glean the nuggets of wisdom that they offer in their area of expertise and choose to ignore the rest.

A Mentor May Answer Only What You Ask

A great mentor will have learned that people only accept imparted wisdom when they are ready and willing to hear it. Only an empty vessel can be filled, and so you must empty yourself of your "wisdom" in order to accept that of others. What this means is that you have to be ready to admit that you don't know everything and that you have a tremendous volume of information yet to learn. A mentor isn't going to take the time to force wisdom down your throat.

The wisest thing you can ask a mentor is, "What do I need to learn in order to move forward?" Another very powerful and very difficult question to ask a mentor is this: "Is there anything about me that is offensive to other people that I am not aware of?" This question requires great courage on your part to ask, because you will likely hear some uncomfortable truths.

Because you are the protégé and you express accumulated wisdom through growth, it means that you must then apply what you have learned and change the very part of you that has been invisible to you. As well as being challenging for you to ask the question, it is challenging for the mentor to answer it. The reason for this is that most people don't want to hear the truth about themselves when they ask this question; what they actually want is for the mentor to simply say, "You don't have to change a thing; you are wonderful as you are." Mentors have likely been burned in the past by answering this kind of question; some people seem to want an answer but become offended when the mentor points out their weaknesses. You must humble yourself and be willing to hear the truth. You must develop an insatiable craving for self-improvement. You must be willing to look directly at the parts of your life that are not satisfactory or fulfilling and make efforts to change them according to your mentor's advice. If you don't ask, the mentor may not be willing to volunteer any constructive criticism.

Action Steps

Creating wealth is potentially the fastest and most exciting game on earth. In order to play this game successfully, you would be wise to follow in the footsteps of those who have blazed a trail of success before you. Decide what your money game will be, and take action to create the prosperity you desire!

1. **PLANNING FUNDAMENTALS.** In developing your plan for wealth creation, have you included all the planning fundamentals we have discussed? Have you determined the promised actions, specific deadlines, milestones and resources that you require? Choose an individual who is trustworthy to review your plans and make suggestions.

2. **WEALTH STRATEGIES.** What can you learn from the stories of successful people? Who do you know who has accomplished a great victory in the area of your focus? What can you learn from their story?

3. **MASTERMIND TEAM.** If you could assemble a dream team, who would be on it? Select a date in your calendar and call a meeting, inviting the key people you wish to associate with. What value can you bring into their lives, just as you hope they will bring value into yours?

4. **MENTORSHIP.** Do you currently have a mentor? If you could be mentored by anyone, who would it be? Is this someone that you currently have a connection with, or is it someone to whom you need to become closer? When will you approach them and demonstrate your willingness to be a good student? Don't just say that you want to be mentored; show that you are humble and willing to receive instruction because you seek self-improvement.

The final chapter in this book is short, but it asks a very important question for you, your family, your community and your legacy: what is your greater purpose?

DESIGN YOUR GREATER PURPOSE

Imagine walking through a forest that is dark from the dense growth of trees. You see sunlight breaking through the trees ahead, and you enter a clearing. The clearing is peaceful and relaxing. A gentle waterfall splashes on one edge, feeding a river that winds lazily past you. The tree branches wave gently in the breeze and the ground is dappled with sunlight. You experience a profound sense of serenity.

But something changes. Tangled weeds spring up from the ground, and not just any weeds: these are the most aggressive, all-consuming weeds you have ever seen. They spread like a plague, choking off the grass until there is none left, crawling up the trunks of the trees and blanketing them until only the foul vegetation can be seen. You watch in horror as it takes only a few moments for this pristine oasis to be clogged and overwhelmed with these unpleasant newcomers. There is no room left in the clearing for any beauty, any new growth; the weeds have claimed all the available space and destroyed the possibilities that might have been created here.

Now, imagine that you are traveling through your life journey and you come into a new situation that seems to be filled with opportunity. Perhaps it's the chance to form new relationships, to start new business ventures, to take control of your emotions or to finally create the body you want and deserve. It seems as if all the baggage of the past has been left behind; it's a fresh start and you can become anything and anyone you want to be. The possibilities are endless! And now imagine that every time you think you've discovered an opportunity like this to grow, discovered this imaginary "clearing" in the forest of your life, imagine that just as you arrive in this clearing it starts to become overrun with weeds. These weeds consume and ruin everything good and beautiful that you discovered, destroying your chance to create something new and beautiful.

Sound like a flight of fancy? You've probably experienced this situation dozens of times, without even realizing it. You start a new relationship, but it fizzles out before long because you've learned from past relationships that you can't really trust people. Maybe you started a new business venture, but it loses steam because you know deep in your heart that you've failed before, and so you assume you're probably just going to fail again. You attend a seminar to take control of your finances but ultimately figure what's the point, you're probably just going to overspend as always. You signed up at a health club to lose weight, but by Friday night you're eating pizza and you've sunk into despair, thinking you'll never really change.

What happens to us when we are enthused about making positive change in our life, and yet we become hampered not from external obstacles but from internal turmoil? What happens is that every time we come into a "clearing," a place in our life where we can make positive change, we carry with us "weeds" (our baggage) from the past that threaten to overrun the scenic beauty of the new experience. And, left unchecked, these weeds will follow us and consume every new opportunity we try to create. If we are to move forward in life, we have to attack the weeds, finally ridding ourselves of them to create a sanctuary where we can experience new and powerful possibilities in our lives.

Create the Sanctuary

CHOOSE WHAT TO BRING WITH YOU

When you walk into a new clearing, it's important to remember that you have company. Everyone who has ever praised you, and everyone who has ever condemned you, is at your side. Every triumphant victory and every heart-wrenching defeat gets dragged along with you into every new situation, and as the years wear on you may discover that you are carrying quite a lot! Some people refer to this as "baggage," particularly in relationships, when a person is unable to move past the sorrow and the disappointment of the past, and so they end up suffocating their future happiness by repeating the same old bad patterns that made their past so unpleasant. Werner Erhard, founder of est and an ontological genius, advises that the way to break this pvattern is to "create your future from your future, not from your past."

So, what baggage are you carrying with you, and have you really made a conscious choice about it? Most people don't choose what they bring with them from their past into the present; their psyche is a hodge-podge of contradictory belief systems and a tapestry of emotional lessons that remain unresolved. When you stand up and do a presentation in front of a business audience, do you bring your greatest cheerleaders on stage with you in your mind, or do you bring the kids in grade 3 who laughed at you during show-and-tell?

Most people bring the bad memories and choose to leave behind the good memories. People are often so focused on their expectations that they miss what is happening in front of them. You expect people to laugh, and so you get what you have imagined: people laugh at you! Why would you do this to yourself? Why would you consciously choose to be a passive victim of the setbacks of your childhood, the heartbreak of your youth, the disillusionment of your adulthood? You must choose to bring only your victories, your celebrations and the moments of empowerment with you into the future. And if you are to bring the ghost of the past with you, please choose to bring only the lessons that you have learned from a setback, or the strength of character you developed by being tested in moments of challenge. There is no value in bringing fear, pain and anger with you into the future. Instead, choose to bring joy, peace and forgiveness into your new clearing.

What are the failures that you feel doomed to repeat, the anguish you feel you deserve to suffer? Understand that this is not the experience of humankind at its ideal. It is not right that you should feel pain. It is right that you feel *elation*. It is right that you feel *freedom*. It is right that you feel *at peace with yourself*. It is right that you feel free to create any new possibility you can imagine. You are meant to operate at the limits of your possibility and then push past those limits to redefine your potential. You are meant to become the greatest version of yourself possible! This is the future to which I want to invite you. Let us resolve to leave behind the darkness of the past and walk toward the sunlight of our new tomorrow.

To reach this new clearing, we must be honest with ourselves about what experiences we have carried forward from our past that continue to shape us. What are the things that people said or did that left a lasting impression? What lessons did you learn about the way people are, the way the world is, the way you are and the way people think you should be? Take a moment and seriously consider what some of your past baggage might be.

Begin by identifying limiting or negative beliefs. We frequently have a passive attitude about things that we believe are out of our control. Because the possibilities for creating our reality are endless, any chains that you believe bind you are usually self-made.

What is it about your life that you just don't believe you can change? Take a moment and brainstorm any limitations you may have in the various areas of your life that you perceive to be an insurmountable obstacle.

Inventory of Limitations
In your marriage: _____
In your career: _____
In your finances: _____
In your family life: _____
In your friendships: _____
In your health: _____
In your emotions: _____
In your self-esteem: _____
In your spiritual life: _____
In your personal time: _____

WHAT DOES "NOT CHOOSING" COST YOU?

If you believe that all these realities have been forced on you, that you didn't choose them, that it's okay to admit you are powerless and that it isn't your fault, then you are cutting off all possibility of creating a new reality. You are eroding all hope and starving all ambition for personal improvement. Your limiting beliefs will sabotage your efforts to create wealth.

If you don't have control over your destiny, who does? Your boss? Your parents? Your spouse? Your friends? The people on the street? The news anchors on television? The movie stars and pop stars you see in commercials? Why would you absolve yourself of the responsibility of leading your own life? As much as other people may have influenced you in the past, you must decide not to simply repeat the past like an automaton. You are not a robot; you are a thinking, feeling being.

On top of that, if you don't choose your life, you have to make up a story justifying why you've allowed bad things to happen. For example, if your parents were drug dealers, you can make up a story that it's not your fault you didn't get all the breaks in life and that's why you're making some mistakes and paying the consequences. Isn't that a great story? By telling yourself this over and over, you'll actually start to believe it and you won't have to feel bad that you didn't choose to pull yourself out of where you are, clear the weeds out and create a better future for yourself. It might seem uncaring and callous that I would say this. I truly mean to bring blessings into your life, so if my words seem uncaring, know that they are actually meant to startle you and get you thinking. Maybe you too have been telling a story to yourself, and you've started to really believe the story. Until you give up the "security blanket" that your story provides you, you can't move on.

Do you have any idea what incredible miracles can occur in your life if you simply choose to create your life? What if you awaken to the possibility that all of your life is *your* creation, that you are the author of your autobiography, that you are the sculptor of your bust? You will realize that with the same ease you can open the doorway to any dream you desire. You can experience an absolute *transformation*. You *must* accept total responsibility for everything in your life. Your marriage? You chose it. Your current income? You chose it. Your weight? You chose it. Your level of happiness? You chose it. Imagine the freedom that this simple understanding will create! Your canvas is blank; you are free to produce.

So when you get passed up for a promotion, say to yourself, "I chose not to get that promotion." When you are stuck in a traffic jam, say, "I chose to be stuck here." You can even laugh at yourself for making these choices! "Why in the world would I do this to myself? Why would I foolishly choose to be in a traffic jam? This was a silly choice." When everything becomes your choice, you are free to choose differently.

STOP THE BLAMING AND CHOOSE FORGIVENESS

Champions create their own reality. They choose their destiny according to their higher values. A champion says things like, "Despite what my mother did, I can choose my destiny. Despite my father's alcoholism, I choose to break the pattern of addiction in my family. Despite my disease, I choose to fully engage life. Despite the economy, I choose to seek prosperity."

Is it possible that you have been the victim of some terrible tragedy, that disaster has befallen you? Absolutely it's possible you suffered through some horrible situations. But blaming the people who did something to you in your past will continue to give them power. Reliving the experience over and over in your mind allows them to live rent-free in your head!

When we forgive someone for their choices to do wrong by us, we are not saying that their behavior is acceptable. We are not condoning their actions. We are not freeing them and saying that they don't need to be held accountable. Forgiveness is a tool that we use, but not to let the other person off the hook; we use forgiveness to let *ourselves* off the hook. To be consumed by anger, when it is our proper right to be lifted by joy, is not my chosen way of being in life. Why would you allow an emotion like anger to define you? Hating another person just consumes your energy and makes you bitter. To paraphrase an adage attributed to Mark Twain, hating someone else and wanting revenge on them is like drinking poison yourself and expecting the other person to die.

When we forgive another person, we relieve ourselves of the anger, bitterness and resentment, and we cast off those feelings like an unnecessary cloak that we were burdened with. You don't need to carry old hurts around; it's exhausting to do so. Give yourself the gift of forgiveness to move past these feelings and clear some space for your future.

GET EXCITED ABOUT YOUR GREATER PURPOSE

The greatest gift you've ever received is the gift of being born. The second greatest gift you'll ever receive is figuring out *why*. Why were you born? Were you born because your dad always dreamed of playing professional football, and now he can live out his fantasy through you vicariously? Were you born because your bank needed to create some profit by selling another 25-year mortgage? Were you born because your company needed someone to answer the phone, close sales deals and manage the part-timers?

You've got to realize that you have every door to every destiny before you, waiting for you to turn the handle and walk through. I find it exhilarating to consider the possibilities of the future. I feel energized just thinking about opening doors to these new possibilities, creating new relationships, closing even bigger deals, stretching myself past my current limits, and learning and growing every day. The thrill of realizing dreams keeps me coming back for more.

We don't discover our purpose by playing small, by holding back or by avoiding personal responsibility — we discover our purpose by going after everything that we want. You don't get to find out who you really are, and what you're really made of, until you come face-to-face with your limits — and try to push past them. You don't get results until you've decided to raise the bar and raise the stakes in your own game. Extraordinary men and women are always redefining what is possible, while average men and women sit on the bleachers of life watching the game that champions play. I'm on the field, playing my game. Are you?

Imagine that your purpose is like the tracks that a train is riding on; it guides you, it focuses your effort, it creates a fast-track toward your ultimate goal. You are the train, your passion and motivation are the fuel that propels your engine forward. Without those tracks to guide you, your energies would be spent in a lifetime pursuit of undefined goals. Your purpose leads to the horizon of your choice; you need only follow your greater purpose and you will be sure to arrive where you dream of.

WHAT IS FILLING YOU UP?

So what are you all about? What makes you tick? Another way of asking this is, "What is filling you up?" If you picture yourself as a vessel or a container, and all the things in your life consume a certain amount of energy, time or space in your soul, what would you find filling up your soul? What do you think about? What are you excited about? What are you worried about? Consider some examples to get you thinking:

- What do you think about late at night?
- What pulls your mind off other things?
- What concerns you?
- What leaves you feeling empowered — or unsettled?
- What are all the areas of your life? (Spouse, kids, house, working out, charity work, the office, lunch with the boss, meeting clients, watching football, etc.)
- What do you spend time thinking about? Worrying about paying the bills, playing with the kids, making a good impression on the boss, saving the planet, protecting animals or making your spouse happy?

Why do we need to concern ourselves with what is filling us up? Because until we clear some of those things out, we won't have room to introduce anything else. An excellent example of this point is the following story. A man approached a monk and asked that the monk grant him all of his wisdom. The monk smiled and offered the man tea. As the monk filled the teacup, he looked directly into the man's eyes and stopped looking at the teacup. In a moment, the teacup was overflowing, and yet the monk kept smiling as he continued pouring tea, and he wouldn't break eye contact. The man shouted, "My tea! You are pouring the tea all over! Foolish man!" The monk, still smiling, said, "Your teacup was already full, so anything else I offered could only spill out onto the table. You need to empty your teacup before I can give you any fresh tea. As well, your teacup is too small for all the tea I have to give. Before I can teach you the wisdom I know, you must first empty your mind or else what I teach you will cause your mind to overflow, and the lesson will be lost. Better still, for me to truly teach you everything I know, you will need to be able to expand your mind so that it is open enough to accept the large volume of wisdom that I will offer you."

The lesson in this parable is simple yet profound: the things that are filling us up are defining us and keeping us from welcoming new truths and possibilities into our life. We have to empty ourselves in order to welcome new potential into our future. And emptying ourselves means, figuratively, getting out of the weeds.

In life, we're going to find ourselves traveling on train tracks toward some kind of horizon. But is it the right horizon? If you say "Forward!" to a monk and a mercenary, they will both obey the instructions, but one will retreat to peaceful seclusion and one will plunge into violent battle. The same directions can mean different things to different people. Are you following someone else's definition of moving forward, or your own?

Why do you get up each day and do the things you do? Have you ever stopped to consider that the reasons you do things are all part of a game that you've been invited to play, but you never consciously chose to play the game of which you are a part? For example, let's say your purpose in life is to win competitions because, deep down, you always wanted your parents' approval. If this is the purpose that drives all your actions, no amount of money or success will ever make you happy; your happiness won't be a variable that you can control. The same will be true if the purpose of your life is to become the CEO of your company because, deep down, you still feel like a scared little kid who was pushed around on the playground by the schoolyard bullies.

Do you recognize that in these hypothetical examples you are bringing your past hurts (the weeds we discussed earlier) into the future, and so any new situation you try to create will automatically be filled up by the weeds of your history? Any time you achieve an accomplishment, it will seem hollow because you'll be looking out into the audience to see if your parents are offering their approval. Every time you try to move forward in your career, you will be paralyzed by the snickers of a group of children from decades ago. You are driven to play a game that other people have designed. I'm here to give you permission to close up that game board and play by your own rules. Create your own purpose!

To break free of a purpose that other people have created, imagine for a moment if you were to continue living your life driven by that purpose. What would be the consequence of doing so? Will you ever feel fulfilled? Will you ever accomplish what you seek? Will you ever acquire what you truly desire? Will you ever connect with the person of your dreams? It may be possible to have some of what you want, but you'll be continuously hampered by the weeds creeping into every new situation.

What would you like to live for? How important is it to you that you are able to create any possibility in your life that you can imagine? I have some good news for you: as soon as you recognize that you've been driven to fulfill someone else's purpose for you, and you decide that you will no longer play the puppet, their power immediately diminishes.

LET YOURSELF BE

If you are truly to master the art of being, you must cast off the self-limiting games, beliefs and actions that you have learned from the people around you. Choose to be at peace with yourself, and open your mind to the idea that you can create any possibility you want, starting from this moment. You already have everything you need inside of you; you need only to clear a space in your future so that you don't repeat the pain of the past.

So clear out the weeds. Clear out the doubt, the embarrassment, the hurts and sorrows, the fears and frustrations, and simply take in the moment. Truly allow yourself to bask in the pleasure of now. Be at peace with who you are, where you are, what you are and why you are. When you quiet your thoughts, you'll realize that all the negative feelings that have plagued you are so easily vanquishable, and you'll laugh at yourself for choosing to carry such a cumbersome burden for so long. All your baggage can simply evaporate and blow away with the wind, leaving you feeling lighter and freer than ever before.

Truly being at peace with yourself means accepting that everything you have done to arrive at this moment was necessary. You don't have to attach any negative emotions to bad memories anymore; you can choose to look at them as dispassionately as you would the two-dimensional stories you read in the newspaper. Being at peace means recognizing that you've chosen to be where you are and who you are. Jean-Paul Sartre said, "Life begins on the other side of despair." I invite you to cast off any lingering despair and move forward into joy.

ARE YOU PLAYING FULL OUT?

In order to be the greatest version of yourself, you must commit fully to the moment at hand. You cannot simultaneously feel elation for your present-day victory if you are hobbled by self-defeating thoughts, for our inner voice becomes a prophecy and we will ensure the prophecy comes to pass by not giving 100 percent in this moment. Are you fully present in what you are doing and what you are being in this moment? Have you given yourself permission to be alive right now, to savor the joy that this moment could offer you, or do you keep playing it safe by repeating old patterns that hold you back?

Committing yourself fully to the moment means clearing your mind of distraction, of the heaviness of fear and anger; clearing your mind so that you are not daydreaming of tomorrow or checking your mobile. Being fully present means that you are totally aware of what is happening now and that you realize the magic in this moment. Every sound is a symphony, every taste is a gourmet banquet, every sight is majestic; your senses are overwhelmed with the magic that the universe can offer you. You realize that you can find absolute happiness right here, right now. Nothing else needs to exist except this moment in order for you to feel utterly fulfilled.

How do you create this? You have to get totally honest with yourself. When you are having a conversation, are you thinking of what to say next when you have a chance to speak? When you are walking down the street, do you savor the feeling of movement or are you in autopilot mode and barely aware of where you are? When you see a person, are they merely an object to be attained or mastered, or are they a kindred spirit who can join you along your journey? Do not permit distraction.

You have to call yourself on the foolishness of your thoughts and actions. You have to get real about the fact that most of the time, you aren't really here — you're back in your childhood or worried about tomorrow. You're rehearsing a speech or replaying a bad movie.

When was the last time you were absolutely committed to being present in your own life? Søren Kierkegaard said, "Most men pursue pleasure with such breathless haste that they hurry past it." Is it any wonder that life loses its luster when we quite literally never stop to smell the roses? But don't just stop to smell them. Marvel in the complexity of so beautiful a creation. Bask in the perfume of the roses, in the silky texture of their petals. Immerse yourself in the mystery of the rose in front of you, savor the delicious flavors of the food you eat and appreciate the beauty of the unique spirits of the people with whom you speak. What a tragedy it would be if you were never actually being present in your own life; what a miraculous gift to yourself it would be if you chose to participate fully in every incredible moment. To quote Kierkegaard again:

The highest and most beautiful things in life are not to be heard about, nor read about, nor seen but, if one will, are to be lived.

Action Steps

We can't achieve the success we desire in life until we have created a clearing that will allow for the manifestation of possibilities. By resolving to address unfinished business, you open the door to a brighter future, one where you are free to manifest whatever you desire.

1. BE RESOLVED. What are the weeds in your forest? What are the pieces of baggage that you carry with you? Resolve once and for all to address these issues. If you need to speak to someone and say what has until now been left unsaid, do so. If you have failed someone, seek their forgiveness. If you have broken your integrity, make amends as best you can.

2. CHOOSE WHAT TO BRING WITH YOU. What do you continue to carry into the future? What choices have been made by other people that have affected you? If you don't consciously choose what to bring into your future, how will not choosing affect you?

3. CREATE SPACE. When an orange is squeezed, out comes orange juice. When you are "squeezed," what comes out? Is it anger? Is it sadness? Whatever is filling you up will be revealed. In order to bring new things into your life, you must create space inside yourself for them. What will you remove?

4. FORGIVE. Choose to forgive those who have wronged you, and release yourself from the burden of anger.

RICHARD DOLAN
ENTREPRENEUR, AUTHOR &
PERFORMANCE STRATEGIST

Since 1995, Toronto-based Richard Dolan has served entrepreneurs worldwide primarily in the fields of merchant bank-
ing, financial services, private client management and real estate
investing. Dolan has coached and mentored corporations, leaders,
entrepreneurs, athletes, politicians, authors, filmmakers and
business owners, producing millions in revenues and billions in
net worth.

ENTREPRENEUR & BUSINESS STRATEGIST A successful entrepreneur, Dolan has served as president to five privately held companies with diverse interests ranging from marketing, branding and
communication to leadership development. He is currently
president of the REIN Group of Companies Inc. and CEO of
The London Academy of Entrepreneurship.

LECTURER Dolan co-authored and presented two certificate
programs for the Schulich Executive Development Centre at
York University: *The Certificate in Marketing and Selling Wealth*

Management Services and *The Certified Wealth Manager*. Today, Dolan continues to lecture regularly on performance, resilience and strategy.

AUTHOR Dolan has written twelve books, many of which bear the Life Rich™ signature, meaning "to live a richer life." He and co-author Dr. Paul G. Stoltz published *Invincible Investor*, which focuses on behavioral finance, happiness economics and investor resilience. In 2015, Dolan published *The Wealth Mastery Playbook: The Six Essential Shifts to a New Financial Destiny* and *Performance: Decoding Human Excellence through Sports Psychology* with co-author David Tod.

AUTHORITY ON PERFORMANCE AND PERFORMANCE PSYCHOLOGY Dolan has collaborated with global brands such as the Miami Heat, Toronto Raptors, Lamborghini, Audi, Pagani Automobili, BMW, Bentley Motors, Callaway Golf, Merck Pharmaceuticals, UPS, Livingson, Marriott Hotels, Sotheby's International Realty, Merrill Lynch, ING Funds, Scotiabank, CIBC, UBS, Royal Bank of Canada, HSBC, Société Générale and BNP Paribas. Dolan was gifted two National Basketball Association championship rings in 2012 and 2013 by player/coach Juwan Howard for his leadership, friendship and contribution.

SPEAKER Dolan has shared the stage with many luminaries, including former US Presidents William Jefferson Clinton and George W. Bush, former President of Mexico Vicente Fox, former Prime Minister of Canada Brian Mulroney, Hillary Clinton, Oprah Winfrey, Tony Robbins, and Sir Richard Branson.

For more information and to book Richard Dolan for speaking or consulting, visit www.richarddolan.com.

NOTES